THE WILD MUSTANG

HORSES OF THE AMERICAN WEST

HISTORY COMICS

THE WILD MUSTANG

HORSES OF THE AMERICAN WEST

Written by
CHRIS DUFFY
Art by
FALYNN KOCH

:01
First Second
New York

Published by First Second
First Second is an imprint of Roaring Brook Press, a division of Holtzbrinck Publishing Holdings Limited Partnership
120 Broadway, New York, NY 10271

Library of Congress Control Number: 2020911022
Paperback ISBN: 978-1-250-17428-4
Hardcover ISBN: 978-1-250-17427-7

First edition, 2021
Edited by Dave Roman
Cover design by Kirk Benshoff and Andrew Arnold
Interior book design by Sunny Lee
Authenticity readers: Rosalyn LaPier and Elise McMullen-Ciotti

Inked in Photoshop with Kyle T. Webster brushes, including the China marker, wet charcoal, pocket brush, and more. Colored digitally in Photoshop.

Printed in China by Toppan Leefung Printing Ltd., Dongguan City, Guangdong Province
Paperback: 10 9 8 7 6 5 4 3 2 1
Hardcover: 10 9 8 7 6 5 4 3 2 1

Growing up in the West Texas town of San Angelo, we heard many stories of the old days—of the cowboys, longhorn steers, and most especially the mustangs. This was, after all, the very town that the famous cowboy novelist Elmer Kelton called home. In time, Mr. Kelton befriended me, and I loved the stories he told of the wild cowboys and the even wilder horses. The annual Stock Show and Rodeo at the San Angelo Coliseum was a highlight of the year for all the local kids. Western television stars often appeared at the rodeo. In those days, we had only one television channel in San Angelo, but it was jam-packed with Western shows about brave cowboys and their wonderful horses. In some cases, the horses were as famous as the cowboy and cowgirl heroes—Gene Autry rode Champion; Roy Rogers galloped across the range on Trigger, billed as the smartest horse in the West, while his wife, Dale Evans, rode Buttermilk; Hopalong Cassidy could always count on his snow-white stallion Topper; Annie Oakley left a trail of dust on her palomino Target, while the Lone Ranger and his Native American companion, Tonto, rode Silver and Scout—and some of these trusty steeds even had comic books devoted to them. Some horses had their own shows: In 1956 alone, you could watch *The Adventures of Champion* (Gene Autry's wild mustang before Gene tamed him), *My Friend Flicka,* about a Wyoming mustang, and, best of them all *Fury,* about a young boy and the black stallion that only he could ride. I thought that everyone must love mustangs as much as I did, but as you will soon discover in this book . . . that has not always been the case.

The name mustang comes to us from the Spanish *mesteño,* meaning simply wild with no master. It was the Spanish, of course, who brought the first horses into what was to become the American West. (The great irony in this was that the ancestor of all horses had originated over fifty million years ago in what we now call North America, before they became extinct, while at the same time thriving and spreading across the continents of Africa, Europe, and Asia.) The return of the horse to the Americas began in 1493, when Christopher Columbus brought at least fifty to the West Indies on his second voyage. In 1519, Hernán Cortés brought sixteen horses on his expedition to conquer Mexico. Spanish reinforcements soon brought even more horses, and they proved instrumental in the destruction of the mighty Aztec Empire.

The largest reintroduction of horses into what was to become the United States began with the 1540 Coronado expedition, but it was Don Juan de Oñate who reintroduced the horse back into the American West. His colonizing expedition of 1598 brought 1,500 horses and mules into what is now New Mexico. When the 1680 Pueblo Revolt briefly expelled the Spanish from their lands, hundreds of horses were captured or ran free. The victorious Pueblo people established a profitable trade in horses with the Comanches, and within a few years, Plains Indian culture was revolutionized as the horse became a central part of tribal life not only in hunting and warfare, but also as a conspicuous sign of social prestige and wealth.

By 1800, there were at least a million wild horses roaming the southern plains, and perhaps more. These great herds attracted the attention of American adventurers, who flouted Spanish law with "mustanging" expeditions into Texas. Their bold exploits captured the imagination of Americans east of the Mississippi River and encouraged American migration into Texas. Before long, the Texas cowboy mounted on a spirited mustang became an American symbol of freedom.

And so the mustang, broken and saddled by Hispanic vaqueros, former slaves turned wranglers, and Anglo cowboys, helped to drive millions of Texas longhorns north up the Chisholm Trail to wild end-of-track cow towns like Abilene and Dodge City. Mustangs also provided much of the stock for the short-lived Pony Express, carrying young Buffalo Bill Cody and other riders over 1,500 miles from St. Joseph, Missouri, to Sacramento, California, in an astonishing ten days. Mounted on their tough mustangs, the Plains tribes battled the U.S. Army for their homelands and brought down Custer and his fabled Seventh Cavalry in 1876, before being swept asunder—by disease, war, and other factors—and confined on reservations. Their vast pony herds went the way of the buffalo as the white man's cattle now spread across the western grasslands from the Canadian border to the Rio Grande.

Until about 1900, there was a ready market for western horses to be used on eastern farms and in the cities, but the coming of the automobile put an end to that. Between 1915 and 1960, the horse population in the United States dropped from 20 million to 4.5 million. In the West, ranchers, with little incentive to round up mustangs for sale and determined to keep every blade of grass for their cattle, began to shoot wild horses. The new world of iron, steam, and asphalt had no place for the mustang.

Then, just when all seemed lost, Velma Bronn Johnston rode to the rescue—just in the nick of time like one of the TV heroines of my youth. A chance 1950 encounter with a slaughterhouse-bound trailer loaded with a number of terrified and injured horses was the initial spark that ignited Velma's fiery crusade to save the mustang. In turn, she battled government bureaucrats, slaughterhouse operators, mustangers, and ranchers who banded together to defeat "Wild Horse Annie," as they derisively called her. Backed by a massive letter-writing campaign from children all across America, Annie stormed the halls of Congress, and in the

face of fierce opposition won passage of the so-called "Wild Horse Annie Act" of 1959, which outlawed the hunting of horses on federal land from motorized vehicles and airplanes. This was but the first in a string of legislative victories that culminated with the Wild Free-Roaming Horses and Burro Act, signed into law on December 15, 1971. This new law made it a crime to harass or kill horses and burros on public land and charged the Bureau of Land Management (BLM) and Forest Service with their protection "as living symbols of the historic and pioneer spirit of the West."

Wild Horse Annie continued the fight for wild horse preservation and protection until her death on June 27, 1977. This child of the New West saved the living symbol of the Old West, and her story is the exciting climax of this book. Her fight continues, and it is up to you to carry on her crusade to save the mustang!

–**Paul Andrew Hutton**,
Professor of History, University of New Mexico

Chapter 1: Meet Lightnin'!

Hi there! My name's Lightnin'.

I'm a ***mustang,*** the fabled wild horse of the American West!

Meet a Mustang

Canada
United States
Mexico
There are wild mustang herds in Arizona, California, Colorado, Idaho, Montana, North and South Dakota, Nevada, New Mexico, Oregon, Washington, Utah, and Wyoming!
Did I mention we're glorious and we run free? Let's see, what else?
Oh, yeah ...

. . . we're also a symbol of *freedom* and America's *wild, untamed spirit!*
Additionally, everybody loves us!
?
Hooray!

Well, that's everything—gotta go now!
♪
RIIIIIIIIP
CHOMP
Oof!
BUMP
?
What's the big idea?
PTOOO!
On your way somewhere?

We finished our book about mustangs! We're gonna go have a little celebration!
TWEEEET
Do you think maybe you left a few things out?
Not likely! I'm a big fan of horses. Would you like to *add* something?
A *few* things, actually . . . like . . .
. . . although it's true that there are about 75,000 wild mustangs roaming freely in the United States today
(and not everyone agrees this is a good thing),
there are also about an *equal number* fenced in.
That may seem like a lot, but about 150 years ago, there were *millions* running wild in the American West—
sometimes in giant herds that took hours to pass a bystander.
Whoa!
SHAKE

And yet, about 500 years ago, there were *zero.*
You are blowing his mind.
POW
Hold on a second . . .
do you have some kind of inside scoop on this whole mustang thing?
Hmm . . .
Big ears?
Really long hair?
Hooves for feet.
I don't get it, what's—

Ah-ha!
You look like a horse!
I mean you *are* a horse!
And a talking one at that.
I'm flattered you noticed.
SLAP
And now . . .

Do you two want to know the ***whole story*** of mustangs?

NOD
NOD
NOD
NOD

Then let's go back to where it started . . .
Oh! Oh!
Probably on the wide-open plains,
the thunder of hoofbeats rumbling in the distance!
. . . on a ship in the Atlantic Ocean!
Oh, now this was unexpected.
This way!

CHAPTER 2: Off the Coast of Hispaniola
It's 1493. That's the GALLARDA, one of 17 small ships on Christopher Columbus's ***second voyage*** from Spain to the New World . . . (well, "new" if you are European).
The king and queen of Spain have charged Columbus with bringing livestock to start a permanent colony. See who's on deck?
Horses! Well, I'll be a monkey's uncle!
Possibly.
But let's listen in . . .
Señor Bermudez! The captain says I'm to help you with the horses today!

I ***will*** need a hand, Señor Arias. We are approaching our destination, and the horses must be readied!
Do we . . . brush them? Clean their feet? Give them a rubdown? I've seen you doing all those things throughout the voyage.

HA! No pampering for them today! We're going to untie the horses from their slings and get them ashore!
Why are they tied up like this? And on deck?

These caravel ships aren't so big, as I'm sure you know! Belowdecks it's ***jam-packed*** with supplies and items to trade with the Natives!
Easy there, big fella!

As for the slings— well, these horses don't have their sea legs!
They'd fall overboard on a rough day! And they say the rolling boat is bad for their bones . . .
!
Whoops! That's another reason they were tied—
they like to ***kick*** at anything behind them!

I hope I can own a horse someday, but they are expensive!
Yes, they are. Except for the *wild* ones!
Wild ones?
Where I come from—a part of Spain called Galicia—there are wild ponies with handsome bushy mustaches (so they can eat the thorny gorse plant)!
They belong to everyone in my village! We round them up once a year and cut their hair for rope . . . we geld the inferior males to make the herd better.
Do you ride them?
If we want a riding pony, *yes!*
We take one from the herd and we break it, that means to *train* it to accept a rider.

So, are these Galician ponies?
What? You're such a city boy!
No—these belong to our mission's big, tough lancers. They wouldn't be caught dead on a little pony!

These stallions are . . . well, let's call them Barbs from Andalusia—strong but light horses with Arabic and North African blood! They're smart and agile—and good jumpers!
They can carry our brave
(and somewhat heavy)
armored soldiers into battle . . .
Hmph!

The Barb
SHORT BACK (the key to good AGILITY)
SLOPING RUMP
SHORT NECK
HEIGHT
13.2 to 15 hands
(53 to 60 inches)
LOW-SET TAIL
ROUND, FULL BODY
Comes in gray, bay, chestnut, black, and brown.

Maybe now I can give this one a brushing? His mane is a bit ruffled!
No time for that! The admiral wants these beasts ashore.
You two big swabs—help us out!

I've seen horses taken off ships at home. But where's the winch? And is there a dock?
No dock, no winch! They ***swim to shore!***
!
What–?
Over the side!
SPLASH

Soon
Whew! That's done! The other ships will be sending their horses over, too—about 35 in all. We'll round them up once we get ashore.
It's rough on the horses, but it's better this way!
Huh? Why?
It'll frighten the Natives! On the first voyage, we saw ***no horses*** in these lands! Giving them a scare with these big brutes will help Admiral Columbus keep the upper hand!
The upper hand?
We're not just here to give them presents, you know! We want them to show us where the riches are—the ***gold,*** boy!
SWIISH
And if they don't . . .
Well, horses give you the advantage in a fight! You're up high on a powerful beast, and you can strike ***down*** at your foes with a big sword . . .
A horse is a soldier's best friend!
Gulp!

Say . . . that's not so nice, what he said.
The Spanish wanted money—gold—from their invasion of the Americas. And yes, they were often ruthless and violent.
In fact, by 1580, the Spanish had taken over the islands of the Caribbean **and** most of the area of modern-day Mexico . . .
. . . even though the Indigenous people there outnumbered the Spanish by a ***lot!***
BLECH
The army of Hernán Cortés, which conquered the powerful Aztec Empire—the most powerful empire in Meso-America in the 15th century—had only about 500 men!
There were between 15 and 30 million Natives living in the Mexico region in 1500 . . . compared to a measly 200,000 Spanish, who arrived over the span of the 1500s.
How did the Spanish conquer it all so fast?
Well, the Spanish brought diseases from Europe that the Indigenous people had no resistance to . . . and the Spanish had more advanced weapons, armor, ***ANNNND*** . . .
Don't say it!
That's right . . . the Indigenous people on the mainland didn't have horses, and like the man said, horses gave the Spanish a ***huge*** advantage in warfare. One Spanish conquistador even called horses their "fortress" in their wars of conquest . . .
Spanish historian Bartolomé de Las Casas estimated that a Spanish soldier on horseback could kill ***1,000*** unarmed Native Americans in an hour.

Yuck.
Sorry.
Okay . . . so there were no horses in North or South America when the Spanish got here?
Right.
That means today's wild mustangs are somehow descended from *tame* horses brought over on ships?
Right.
Hmm—so we humans may be kind of greedy. (And violent.) But we're good for one thing!
What's that?
Transportation!
Without humans, and our awesome ships, you'd *all* be stuck in Europe!
Yessiree, you needed a ride and *we* gave it to you.
Welcome
EUROPE
THE AMERICAS
Whatever—
we were in the Americas *way* before people.
POOF
CHOMP
But you said—!!!

Sounds like we might need a little ***background break*** ...
What does ***that*** do?
POP
BOOP
Mane Idea 1: Horse Migration!
VMMMMM
Mane Idea 1: Horse Migration!
Corny title.
Horses (known to scientists as *Equus ferus caballus*) actually evolved ***in*** North America . . .
Hey, some wild horses! (At last!)
. . . these are actually some equids (mammals of the horse family) that predated *Equus ferus caballus*. (Not all these relatives of mine lived at the exact same time, but all lived in North America during the Miocene epoch—25 to 5 million years ago!)
Pliohippus
Merychippus
Hipparion
Parahippus
Anchitherium
Dinohippus—closest ancestor to the modern horse!

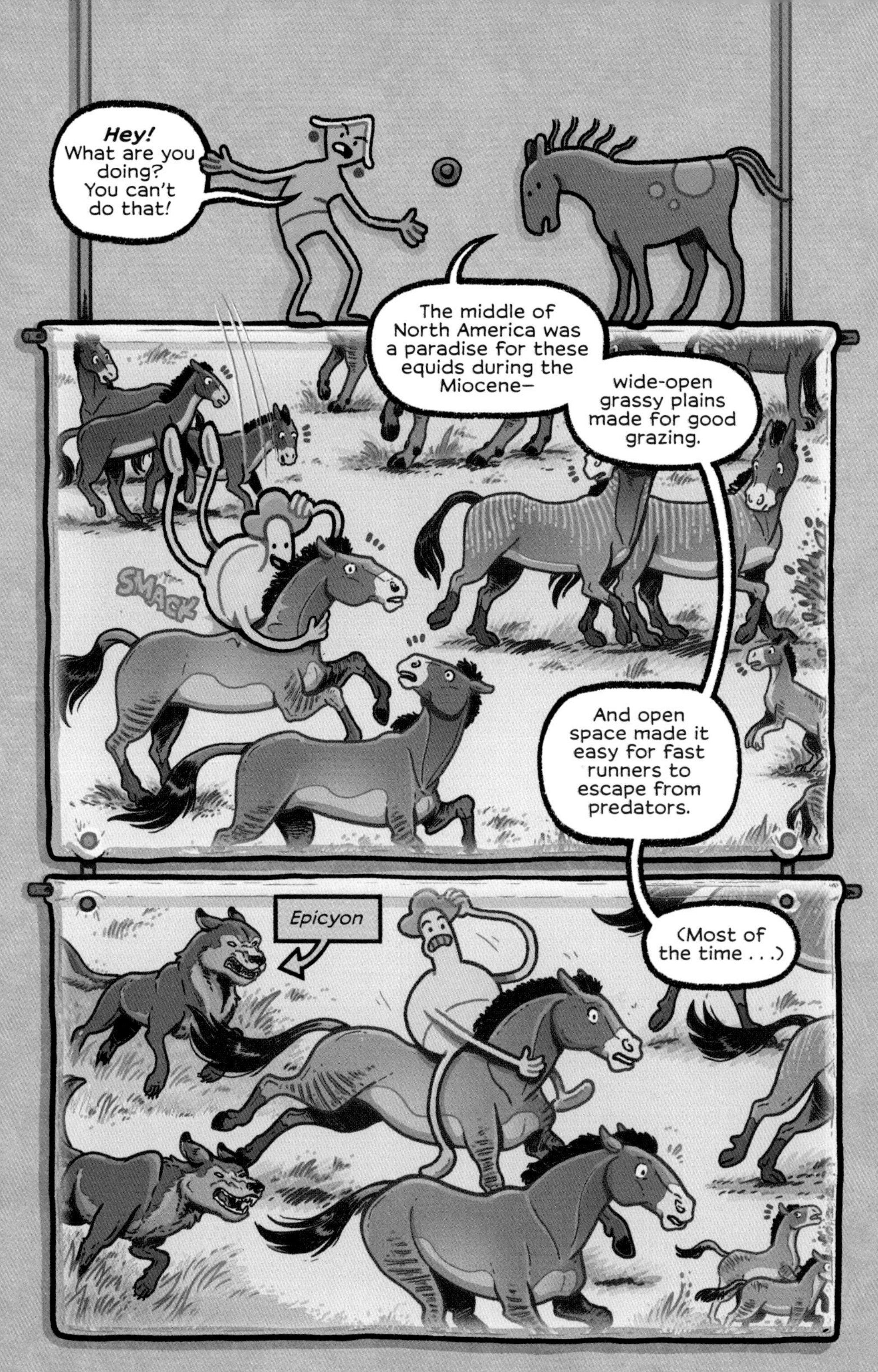

Hey! What are you doing? You can't do that!
The middle of North America was a paradise for these equids during the Miocene—
wide-open grassy plains made for good grazing.
SMACK
And open space made it easy for fast runners to escape from predators.
Epicyon
(Most of the time . . .)

Over millions of years, lots of these equids followed the grassy plains up to a region known as Beringia . . .
How come ***he*** gets to go to Beringia?!
. . . and over to Asia and Europe, which also had lots of grasslands at this time.

They made their way from Siberia . . .
. . . all the way down to . . .
. . . Spain . . .
. . . which is where Columbus's ships sailed from.
Horses!
They're ***world travelers!***
The trip from Spain, of course, happened ***much*** later . . . and by then a new type of equid (the modern horse) had hoofed its way over from North America.
Keep in mind a few things.
This happened over millions of years.
All the equids didn't leave North America, but rather they ***spread out*** across many continents.
Lots of ***other*** animals traveled this way from North America to Asia, and vice versa.

I get it. Horses started in North America. But then why ***weren't*** there some horses in North America when the Spanish showed up?
Well, about 11,000 years ago, the world warmed, and the polar ice caps melted a lot. (Not the first or the last time this would happen.)
The ocean levels rose, most of Beringia went underwater . . .
HUFF HUFF
. . . and no more horses (or any land animals) could travel between Asia and North America.
SPLASH
OH . . . and by the way, humans had been coming over from Asia around this time, too!
!!!
Wow! We just made it! Say, what's to eat around here?
SPLASH

MASTODON
GIANT BEAVER
GROUND SLOTH
YUKON WILD HORSE
HUFF HUFF
Just a little later (around 10,000 years ago), horses, other equids, and most very large mammals (called megafauna) in North America went extinct—
possibly because of rapid climate change.
Or . . . it might have been due to those hungry human hunters who showed up. Scientists don't know which was the cause—it could have been due to both!
What?! Those humans might have . . . eaten horses?
It's not my idea of a good time, either. But we have to get back to the story of mustangs . . .
End of Mane Idea 1
Hmf, did you have a good ride?
PRESS

CHAPTER 3: Going North
Okay, remember the Spanish in New Spain (the area today called Mexico)?
Well . . . around 1600, the Spanish, driven by the desire for mineral wealth and to spread the Roman Catholic religion . . .
. . . sent priests and soldiers *north*, to the area that today is the state of New Mexico.
Havasupai
Hopi
Tiwa
Jicarilla
Tewa
Towa
Santa Fe
Navajo
Keres
Pecos
Mojave
Zuni
Piro
Yavapai
Maricopa
Coyotero
Mimbreño
Yuma
Cocopa
Chiricahua
Mescalero
Papago
Akimel O'odham
New Spain
Apache
Pueblo
Various
There were many Indigenous people *already* living in these areas.
Naturally the Spanish brought horses with them and–
And, that's how we got mustangs, right?! Spirit of wildness and independence!
Run free, Lightnin'!!!
Not quite yet.
Oh.

But soon! The first major Spanish outpost far to the north of New Spain was a town called Santa Fe. The Native peoples of the area were (and are) collectively known as the Puebloans.
Life for the Puebloans under Spanish rule was . . . very hard.
Yay, humans (again).
The Spanish forbade the Puebloans from practicing their own religion, forced them to pay tribute in crops, labor, and textiles—and enslaved or mutilated those Pueblo who didn't obey.
Also, the Spanish *didn't* allow them to ride horses.
Really!
Yes.
Okay, smarty-hoofs . . . then what's *that kid* doing?
Outside Santa Fe, 1610
Hyah!

Ah, Welai . . . good to see you hard at work.
Tending *your* sheep.
I've had a long day. Lots of business at the Palace of Governors.
Okay.
The governor wants us to crack down on you crafty Puebloans.
Apparently, despite the ban on Puebloans learning to ride horses, a lot of you are riding horses! We'll be putting a stop to *that*!
Oh?
Yes, and, by the way, Welai, you must ride out to the ridge before sunset—
I saw some stray sheep up there!
!!??

I guess your job is safe!
Lucky me.
That's right— though the Spanish had made laws against Native Americans riding horses from the start of their time in the Americas . . .
. . . they *also* had many Native servants and slaves tending to their horses. So these laws were broken a lot.
In fact, the king of Spain soon made it legal for Native American servants in Santa Fe to learn to ride.
One question . . .
POKE
Yes?

What's all this got to do with mustangs, which are *wild* horses, right?!
Tame
WILD
In answer to your question . . . I direct your attention to . . .
. . . the *Pueblo Revolt!*

Whoa! I guess the Puebloans got tired of being mistreated?
Yes, the Native peoples drove all the Spanish out of the Santa Fe area in 1680. It was violent and hundreds of people were killed—but most Spanish were allowed to leave the region in peace.
The Pueblo took most of the Spanish horses. It was the largest transfer of horses into Native American possession up to this time. Luckily, the Pueblo knew how to take care of them . . .

I think I see where this is going. The horses all escaped and became wild, right?
Not exactly . . .
. . . a few probably escaped,
but the Pueblo kept most of them to trade with other Native tribes.
TWEEEEET
TIME-OUT!
We'd like to express our disappointment.
It was our understanding that this is a book about mustangs and wild horses!
GRAPHIC NOVEL REVIEW COMMITTEE

I know. Trust me, we're getting there.
When?
How?
The Spanish keep 'em corralled, the Puebloans keep them to trade ...
I know! Maybe a few strays wandered into the wild and over time reproduced and created the ***vast herds of wild horses!***
That's a theory a lot of historians had.
Yes, yes! I ***like*** this theory. (I must be a historian!)
Unfortunately, it's incorrect. There's no way you'd get the huge number of wild horses that roamed North America from just a few strays.
Then how ... did we get ... all the wild horses ...?
WUMP
GRAPHIC NOVEL REVIEW COMMITTEE
The answer, or the ***key*** to the answer ...

Say, those guys are good horse riders.
. . . is the Comanche.
CHAPTER 4:
The Comanche and Horses— A Love Story of the Plains
Thanks to the Comanche Nation, and later other Indigenous people of the North American plains, there would soon be *millions* of horses in the West.
Well then— let's get to it, before he shakes apart!
ENTHUZZZZIASM

Okay. Here's how it happened.
The Comanche were once part of a different Native tribe, the Shoshone,
who hunted buffalo on the north-central Great Plains.
Shoshone
Comanche
New Spain
Around 1680, the Shoshone split, and the group that would become the Comanche began to move south . . .
There are probably many reasons why they went south . . . to get away from certain other tribes, to escape outbreaks of disease . . .
. . . and some historians think they were enticed by stories of ***strange creatures*** to the south.
?
Strange creatures?! What—?!
From down south, where the Puebloans lived . . . The Spanish had brought these creatures north from New Spain . . .
Um.
. . . they have ***hooves*** and go ***NEIGH-NEIGH?!***
Oh*!* The creatures were horses*!*
Moving right along . . .

The Comanche got horses and they ***loved*** 'em!
Cuz you guys are so cute!
Yes, plus . . .
horses changed ***a lot of things*** for the Comanche.
Before horses, dogs were the Comanche's (and all the Native Americans') only domesticated animal that did any ***work***!
Dogs were often used as pack animals, dragging load-bearing frames called travois when villages were on the move.
(The Comanche tended to move to where the buffalo were at any given time.) . . .
75 lb (maximum)
What a drag . . .
50 lb (maximum)
After horses, the Comanche could move ***more*** of their belongings faster!
300 lb (maximum)
200 lb (maximum)
I ***still*** have to do this?

50 miles in a day (maximum)
HUFF
PANT PANT
125 miles in a day (maximum)
OMPH!
WHIZZZ
YIPE!
Before horses, Comanche could only travel by foot.
After they had horses, they could go much faster—and farther!
And the biggest way it affected their lives was how it changed the way they hunted—
Wait, I know what those are! Buffalo!
Also known as the ***American bison.***
The Great Plains bison were the main source of food—and an important source of clothing and building material—for the Comanche and for ***all*** the Plains people.
Huh. They're just kind of sitting around. I thought they stampeded and stuff like that.

COUGH
COUGH
RUMBLE
Yes, they do stampede . . .
. . . if they have a good reason to!
By the way: There were more than 40 million American bison on the plains until well into the 19th century. (It's hard to determine the exact number since not many people at the time were counting bison for a living . . . but it could have been as many as 80 million!)
Whoa.
This strikes me as a ***very effective*** hunting technique!

Yes, that's a buffalo jump, a hunting method used by many Peoples of the Plains.
But look closer.
Hey! Who's that guy?
He's the *decoy!* A young man would disguise himself as a buffalo calf and, over many miles, try to lead a herd of bison to a preplanned spot . . . a corral or a cliff!
This could be *very* risky! Buffalo could figure out the ruse and charge the decoy . . . and if the plan worked, the decoy would have to take pains to not go over the cliff!
SNIFF
SNIFF
I'm a distressed buffalo calf— follow me, everyone!
This method (and others like it) involved dozens—if not hundreds—of participants—
and one "lucky" decoy.
No, really! I'm a buffalo calf!!!

With the added speed and height that came with horseback riding, the Comanche
(and later all the Peoples of the Plains)
developed *new* hunting techniques.
With their horse matching the speed of a buffalo (and while holding on to their horse with their legs only) . . .
. . . riders would loose arrows, one after another, until a target buffalo fell. (They also used long lances sometimes.)
PLONK PLONK PLONK
With horses, the Comanche could hunt over a wider territory with fewer hunters. (And they didn't have to use decoys as much!)
Phew!

For these reasons and more, during the 1700s, horses became the ***stars*** of the Comanche world.
(Thanks for the spotlight.)
That looks like a lot of work!
Everyone in a Comanche tribe helped take care of horses.
Teenage boys herded the horses to and from pastures.
Women guarded them, and also made horse saddles and packs.
The men planned long-term movements of the herd, trained horses, and . . .
Well . . . we'll get to their ***other*** big job later.
SQUINT
Now that you're a big star, you think you can keep secrets, *huh*?
(*Um*, you can turn the spotlight off.)

By the early 1800s, the average Comanche family had 15 to 20 horses. Some owned as many as 300—and it was not unheard of for the most successful Comanche to own more than 1,000!
Horses were their major trading commodity, a sign of personal wealth, and a source of group pride!
YEAAA!
Comanche kids learned to ride from a very early age.
Many of their games revolved around horses—so there was also a lot of trick riding . . .
. . . and racing! (And betting on races.)
Psst. Two yo-yos and a candy bar say the patchy one wins.
NOD NOD
RUB RUB

They decorated their horses with symbols for hunting, for war, and . . .
. . . and cut that out.
Speaking of war . . .
. . . horses made the Comanche a formidable nation—on horseback they were feared warriors.

Comanchería around 1800
Crow
Cheyenne
Shoshone
Arapaho
Rocky Mountains
Pawnee
Missouri River
United States
Kiowas
Big Timbers of the Arkansas
St. Louis
Colorado River (west)
Sangre de Cristo Mtns.
Osages
Taos
Comanchería
Arkansas River
Mississippi River
Santa Fe
Canadian River
Panismahas
New Mexico (territory of New Spain/ Mexico)
Sabine River
Colorado River (east)
Apache
Pecos River
Brazos River
Trinity River
Lipan Apache
New Orleans
New Spain (Mexico, starting in 1821)
Rio Grande
Tejas (territory of New Spain/ Mexico)
San Antonio
Gulf of Mexico
Towns and Forts
Comanchería
The Comanche used their horse skills to keep unwanted intruders (Native American and European) out of their territory (called the *Comanchería*) for about 150 years!
As uncontested lords of the Southern Plains, the Comanche shaped the future of North America by blocking Spain (later Mexico, when it gained independence)
from moving north to the Great Plains. (It was too dangerous to enter most of the time!)
WHAP!
WHAP!
TUG
Wow! The Comanchería is really big.
And dark.

Towns and Forts
Comanchería
In fact, during the height of Comanche power, Spain, France, Texas, the United States, and every Native American tribe bordering on the Comanchería had to either pay tribute to the Comanche (give them a lot of free stuff) or be at war with them . . . sometimes ***both!***
PAT PAT
The Comanche sound pretty tough—
thanks to you guys!
TUG
So, when do we see the wild—
Comanchería
All the Indigenous people of the Great Plains hunted buffalo and ***every*** tribe saw the advantages to owning horses. Word traveled fast along trade routes up and down the plains.
Once the news got out, everyone had to have horses—and who had the most horses to trade northward on the Plains?
FWIIIP
BLINK BLINK
I get it—the Comanche! But how did the wild h—
Time for another big map!

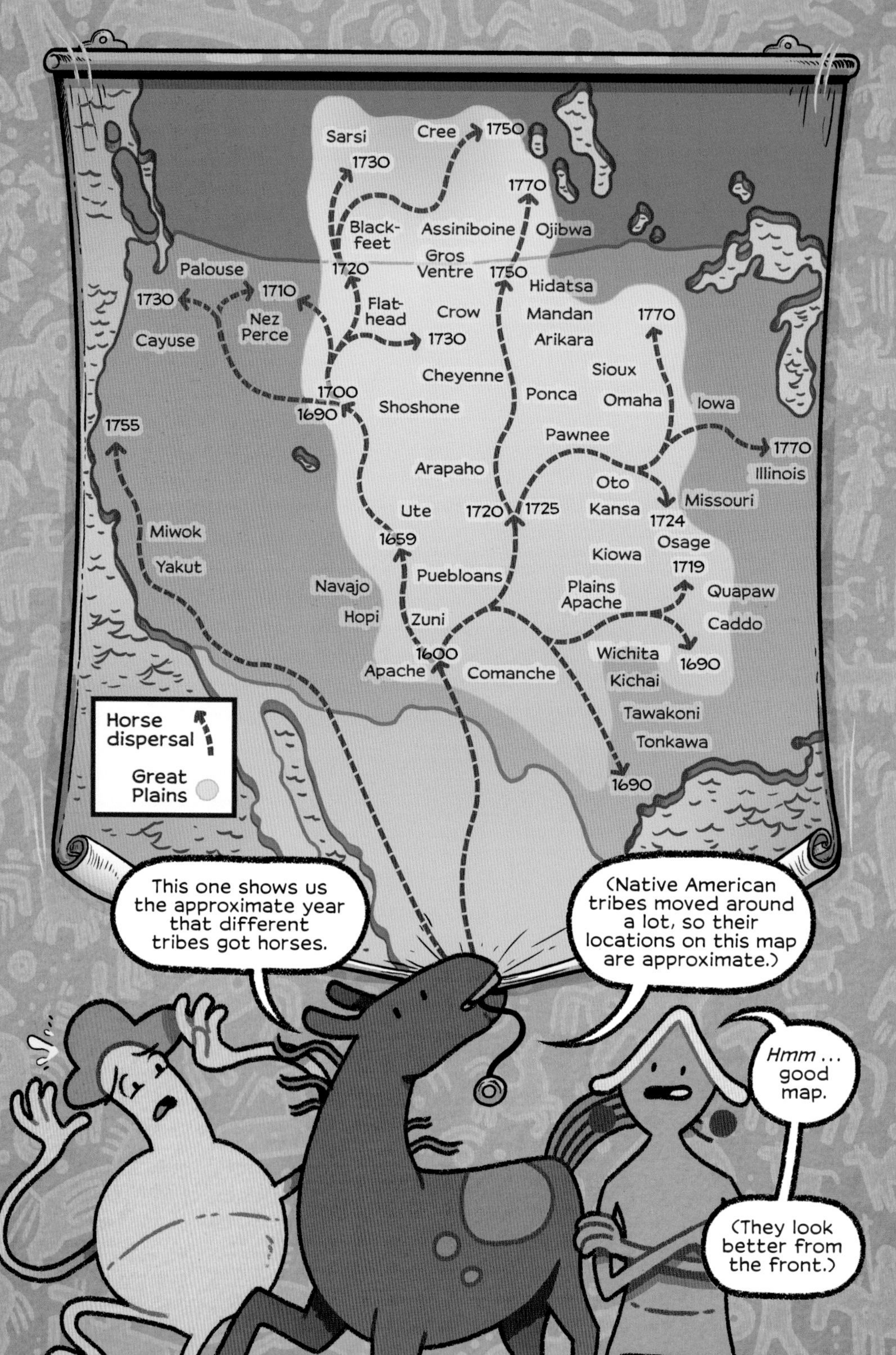

Sarsi
Cree
1750
1730
1770
Black-feet
Assiniboine
Ojibwa
Gros Ventre
1720
1750
Palouse
1730
1710
Nez Perce
Flat-head
Crow
1730
Hidatsa
Mandan
Arikara
1770
Cayuse
Cheyenne
Sioux
1700
1690
Shoshone
Ponca
Omaha
Iowa
1755
Pawnee
1770
Illinois
Arapaho
Oto
Missouri
Ute
1720
1725
Kansa
1724
Miwok
1659
Osage
Kiowa
Yakut
1719
Navajo
Puebloans
Plains Apache
Quapaw
Hopi
Zuni
Caddo
1600
Apache
Comanche
Wichita
1690
Kichai
Tawakoni
Tonkawa
1690
Horse dispersal
Great Plains
This one shows us the approximate year that different tribes got horses.
(Native American tribes moved around a lot, so their locations on this map are approximate.)
Hmm ... good map.
(They look better from the front.)

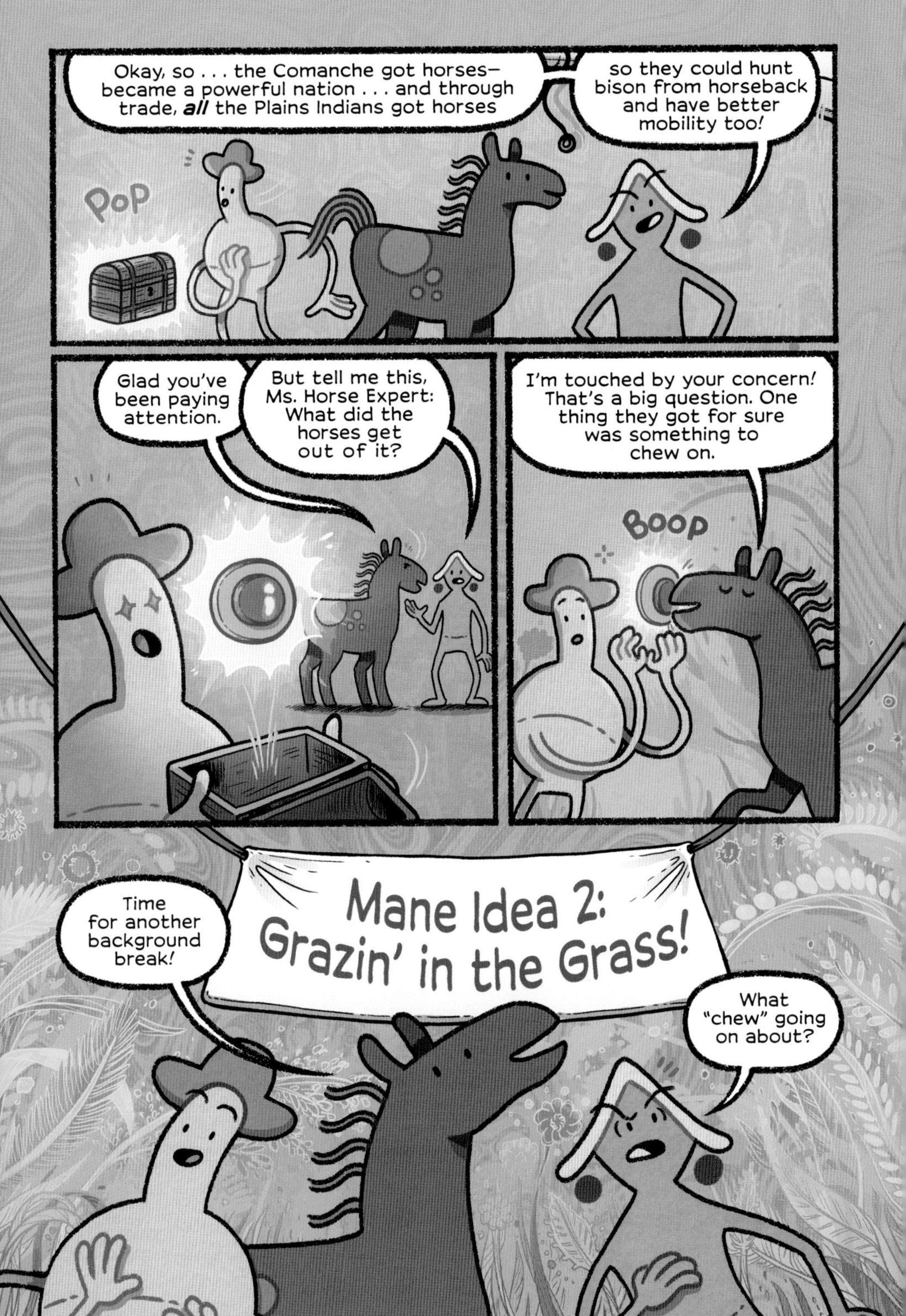
Okay, so . . . the Comanche got horses—became a powerful nation . . . and through trade, ***all*** the Plains Indians got horses
so they could hunt bison from horseback and have better mobility too!
POP
Glad you've been paying attention.
But tell me this, Ms. Horse Expert: What did the horses get out of it?
I'm touched by your concern! That's a big question. One thing they got for sure was something to chew on.
BOOP
Time for another background break!
Mane Idea 2: Grazin' in the Grass!
What "chew" going on about?

By bringing the horse to the Plains, the Comanche and other Plains tribes had returned the horses to the grassy plains of North America from *whence* they originated!
POKE
Nice use of "whence," but we went over this before.
We did . . . however we did ***not*** discuss the connection between grass and horses!
Oh yeah, you ***eat it!*** End of story!
Whoa there!
Horses and grass are linked—and it's part of the story of mustangs and their survival.
Today, all horses like to chomp grass. Their taste for grass really kicked in around 15 million years ago, during the Miocene era.
Eohippus, 50 million years ago
Before that, though, earlier horses (aka equids) had lived in forested areas and browsed for fruit, leaves, and tender plants.
For that job, horses chewed with small narrow teeth.
Eohippus tooth
But during the Miocene, the world got a ***lot*** drier, forests shrank, and new types of grasses replaced the forests. Soon, grass was all there was on the menu in many places.
Hmm
>sniff, sniff<
Smells good . . .
Breakfast: Grass.
Lunch: Grass.
Dinner: Grass.
Dessert: Hope you like grass!

Grass >munch munch< is surprisingly tough! To eat it, you don't chew it. After you bite off a mouthful, >munch munch< you have to grind it (in a side-to-side motion—observe my jaws)! >munch munch<
Horses that thrived in the new grassy world had >munch munch< thick, wide teeth for efficient grinding. Say, this is pretty good! >munch munch<
Grass has silica—like tiny bits of sand—in it, so grinding grass wears teeth down. >munch munch< As a result, the horses that survived this era of grass diets also had long teeth. >munch munch<
Rike riss?
Ah, no. Horses developed long ***molars***—back teeth that do most of the grinding.
They can be up to five inches long, but most of each tooth is inside the gums. The teeth drop down slowly over a horse's lifetime . . . allowing their molars to grind grass for ***decades!***
Conveniently Located X-Ray Machine

Our guts learned a few tricks once grass took over, too.
Horses have a large digestive chamber known as the *cecum* that allows us to eat foods that are *less* nutritious
and often too tough for other animals to digest.
Yup, like grass!
RECTUM
SMALL COLON
LARGE COLON
SMALL INTESTINE
ESOPHAGUS
ANUS
STOMACH
CECUM
Bigger Conveniently Located X-Ray Machine
But the cecum extracts fewer nutrients from food than do the stomachs of ruminants, like cows.
As a result, wild horses around the world can live on a wide variety of barely edible plants . . . but we have to graze pretty much all the time. (17 hours a day!)
Sagebrush
Thistle
Bulrush
Gorse
Beach grass
Poison ivy
Lots of grasses

End of
Mane Idea 2
OMPH!
So the plains were a paradise for us grazers . . .
and it could feed a lot of us.
PRESS
Hmm . . .
Well, I guess that's cool?
MMHM
FLOSS
FLOSS
KRUMPLE

2 PTS
End of
But who cares about teeth?!
Well, dentists, biologists, and probably forensic—
You ***still*** haven't said ***one word*** about wild horses, and we're on, like,
page 200
or something!
BOUNCE
It's only page 50.
SPRITz
SSSSSSS
Hmm . . . ***maybe*** this next chapter requires some . . . expert knowledge. Someone with a special touch.
I'll be taking a little break for now, and I leave you with . . .
???

STEALO THE GREAT
Greetings, humans!
It is *I!* ***STEALO THE GREAT!***
Who–?
Stealo, did you see where our friend went?
She's a horse about your size and–
Stealo does not have time for such concerns...
Stealo must teach you how wild horses thrived in North America thanks to the magic of...
Of?
Stealing!

CHAPTER 5: Horse Raiding as History!
Stealo, you seem like a cool horse and everything, but . . .
stealing . . .
is BAD!
Perhaps, but, because of stealing, North America became home to great herds of wild horses!
I may be willing to reconsider my opinion.
Hey!
To begin this chapter, let's look in on a historical scene that illuminates many things (and includes some excellent stealing!).
Now, allow me to steal you away–
–to 1821!

Stealo presents to you a scene on the banks of the Arkansas River. The area is known as Big Timbers.
Today it's part of southeast Colorado.
A group of about 20 white men are coming from the northeast.
You have learned about the Comanche, yes?
Sure!
By 1821, this area was at the northwestern frontier of the Comanchería.
Here, people of many different tribes would gather for trading as winter approached.
Right now, it's only a group of Kiowa . . .
Hmm . . . We should ride out and meet them!
They may ***need*** a few friends in this place!
Do we give them the regular greeting?
Yes!

RUMBLE
RUMBLE
Colonel Glen! Those Indians are charging at full speed!
What do we do?

SCREECH

Welcome!
PHEW
HEH
SNIFF SNIFF

Come with us to the Winter Trading Village!
You will be guests of the Kiowa (that's us)!
It's close!
And we'll give you a safe place to keep your horses!
Oh, okay!
Hmm, not much of a village!
Just wait . . .
The next day!
Wow! It's like a whole city now!
Many tribes come here: Comanche, Arapaho, Cheyenne, Shoshone, Apache, and us, the Kiowa!
Looking to do any trading?
We have horses, buffalo robes, horses, and also horses!
Well, actually . . .

Stealo is obliged to inform you that this scene is a retelling of events from *The Journal of Jacob Fowler* (1821–22). All dialogue is made up but based on real events. Stealo also advises you that events of several days have been compressed into just a few pages here. Also: Apologies! The numbers of horses ***stolen*** may be somewhat exaggerated by the characters. But they usually are!!

You should also apologize for the name "Stealo."

Mr. Fowler?
Yes, Douglas?

Um . . . well, myself and some of the men were huntin' for meat just now out on the plains . . . and we met up with some Crow who had 200 stolen Arapaho horses . . .
Hmf.
And they kind of . . . convinced us to trade nine of them horses for some gunpowder . . .
Oh!

Um, then some Arapaho surrounded all of us and stole half the Crow horses— and we skedaddled out of there quick. And . . . um . . . we left the nine horses behind.
I see . . .

Oh . . .
and . . .
Yes???

. . . we found out that seven of our horses were stolen from the village pens since we've been here . . .
. . .

Didn't you say this was a ***"trading"*** village?
SHRUG

Ha, ha! More like a ***stealing*** village*!* Am I right?
Stealo ***knows!*** *Ha, ha!*
Stealo, you're kind of corny.

I get the picture. The Native Americans of the Great Plains stole horses from each other a lot. But one thing I don't get . . .

Why steal? You said that they did a lot of horse trading.
You question the value of stealing, *eh*?

The less exciting answer is . . .
sometimes they needed to!
Many tribes needed horses for their new way of life. If they couldn't trade, they went on horse raids. This wasn't seen as stealing in the modern sense. It was more of a military action, and Indigenous people didn't consider it to be a crime, but a positive action that benefited their community.

But ***more*** exciting . . . the raids were a way for young men to show their skill, their cunning, their bravery.

Swiping another group's prize horse out from under their noses gave you and your tribe ***bragging rights!*** Sneaky stealing was highly respected—especially if no one got hurt!

And ***someone's*** about to get hurt!

Stealo admires your bravery, but you need to work on the sneaking.
NOD
NOD

Please allow Stealo to tell you about one of my favorite ***sneaky horse heists!***

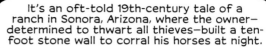

It's an oft-told 19th-century tale of a ranch in Sonora, Arizona, where the owner—determined to thwart all thieves—built a ten-foot stone wall to corral his horses at night.
An iron gate and iron padlock were, he ***thought,*** further guarantors of security.

One night, a stealthy group of Apache scaled the wall . . .

. . . found the best horses . . . and then just waited on horseback.
ZZZ
ZZZ
ZZZ

In the morning when the ranch workers unlocked and opened the gate, the Apache just raced out on their chosen horses! ***Ha!***

Stealing was also **good business!**
The more horses you had, the more you had to **trade** with!

For example, the Comanche traded horses for **bread, corn, guns, kitchen utensils,**
cloth, red paint, and **metal**—all things they had no direct access to.

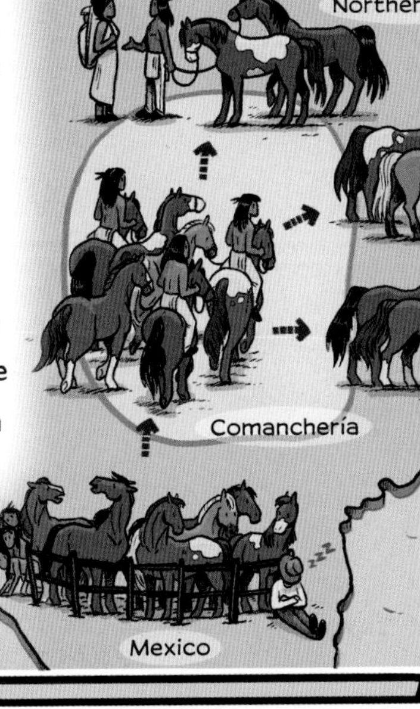
Also driving all this stealing was the **huge demand** for horses from the Indigenous people to the north—
and from the United States to the north and east!
And where could the Comanche, the Apache, and other tribal nations of the Southwest find a rich supply of fresh horses to trade north and east?
Northern Plains
United States
Comanchería
Mexico
Why, in Mexico and Texas!

The Apache and Comanche raided Texan and Mexican ranches with such frequency that those regions were sometimes left with almost **no horses** at all . . .
. . . until ranchers could get more from the south . . . these new horses would often be stolen and traded north, **too!**
NO HAY CABALLOS
Aw, they're out of horses.
Let's come back later . . .

The demand (and high price) for horses in and around the plains led to some ... shall we say ...
big-time heists.
Old Spanish Trail
Salt Lake
Denver
Death Valley
Santa Fe
Los Angeles
Around 1840, a southwestern gang of criminals called Los Chaguanosos had their eyes on the ***thousands*** of horses in ranches in California (then part of Mexico).
Led by African American Mountain Man Jim Beckwourth, Ute master thief Chief Wakara, and former U.S. scout Thomas "Pegleg" Smith . . .
Jim Beckwourth
Chief Wakara
Thomas "Pegleg" Smith
... the multinational gang (consisting of Native Americans, Americans, Mexicans, and French Canadians) stole more than 3,000 horses on a single excursion into California!

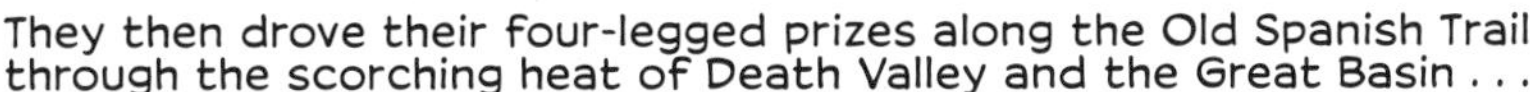
They then drove their four-legged prizes along the Old Spanish Trail through the scorching heat of Death Valley and the Great Basin . . .

. . . ending up near Santa Fe . . . where the price for horses was ***much higher*** than in California.
A long, dangerous journey . . .

but a good investment!
It's considered by many to be the ***largest horse raid in North American history!***
Wait, did they really lie down in a pile of coins and—
No questions! Stealo has a bonus horse-stealing fact for you!

The last horse raid made by a Native American occurred many years later . . .
. . . in Germany during the final days of World War II!
U.S. Army corporal Chief Joseph Medicine Crow (of the Crow Nation) stampeded the horses of German officers holed up in a farmhouse!

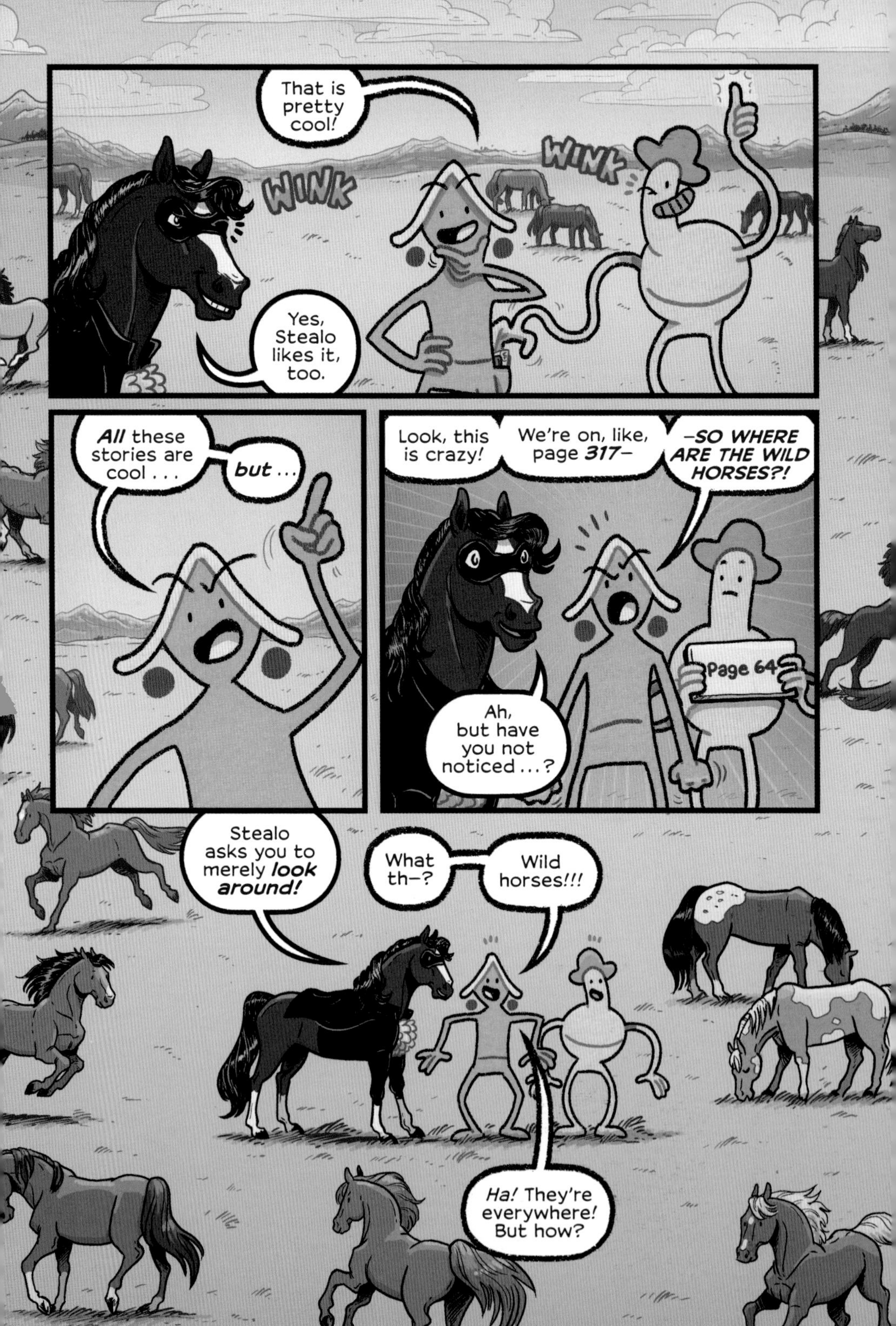
That is pretty cool!
WINK
WINK
Yes, Stealo likes it, too.
All these stories are cool . . .
but . . .
Look, this is crazy!
We're on, like, page 317–
–SO WHERE ARE THE WILD HORSES?!
Page 64
Ah, but have you not noticed . . . ?
Stealo asks you to merely look around!
What th–?
Wild horses!!!
Ha! They're everywhere! But how?

My friends . . . Take it from Stealo: If you ***steal large amounts of anything*** and you try to get away fast, you're gonna lose some loot!
Such was the way with horses, too!
I get it!
Out on the plains, Native Americans, the Spanish, the Mexicans, and the encroaching Americans all had to let their horses roam ***free*** to graze.
Have you learned that we horses need to roam large areas to get enough to eat?
ACK!
BUCK
You see our digestive systems and teeth—
Oh! ***Please stop!*** We learned that already . . .
Oomph
WUMP
Horses grazing on the open plains might get stolen, wander off . . .
. . . or fall victim to the ***greatest horse thieves of all!***
Wait, what? Who . . . ?
Other horses!
Specifically: ***stallions!***

Stealo himself will do one of these now!
Mane Idea 3: Social Structure of Wild Horses!
SMACK!
BOOP
Hmm . . . Okay, but no dental talk.
Horses are ***social creatures***—we ***love*** and ***need*** each other's company. We make lifetime friendships and help each other out!
SWISH
SWISH
Using tails to keep biting flies off each other's eyes!
We live and travel in ***bands***—groups of about 3 to 30. (***Herds*** are a number of bands that share a common territory.)
Bands are usually made up of one stallion (male horse), several mares (female horses), and their young.
A band will follow one alpha (leader) mare, who guides them to different grazing areas.

When young mares and stallions are between one or two years old, they are driven off—and have to form their ***own bands.***
Very funny, my friend! Stealo is laughing on the inside!
WANTED: Horse for band ... must play drums and love the Stone Ponies
After being driven from his herd, a young stallion's goal is to become lead stallion for a new herd of mares.
He'll compete for this role with other bands' stallions. The fights can get pretty ***rough!***
But sometimes he ... guess what?
Let me guess.
Sometimes he ***steals*** them.
VERY GOOD!

Yes, where humans allow tame horses to graze in the open . . .
WINK
. . . mares are often lured away by the charms of a ***wild stallion.***
So you see–
never underestimate the ***romantic powers*** of a handsome master thief!
Hoo boy . . .
TOO FAR!
End of Mane Idea 3
Stealo, don't take this the wrong way, but I miss our ***horse expert*** from before.

Stealo understands.
And what's more . . .
UNZIIIIP!
. . . it was me all along!
Whaaat?
Wow! You really had us fooled!
I can get lost in a role . . .
. . . but you may be relieved to know that we're done with Stealo.

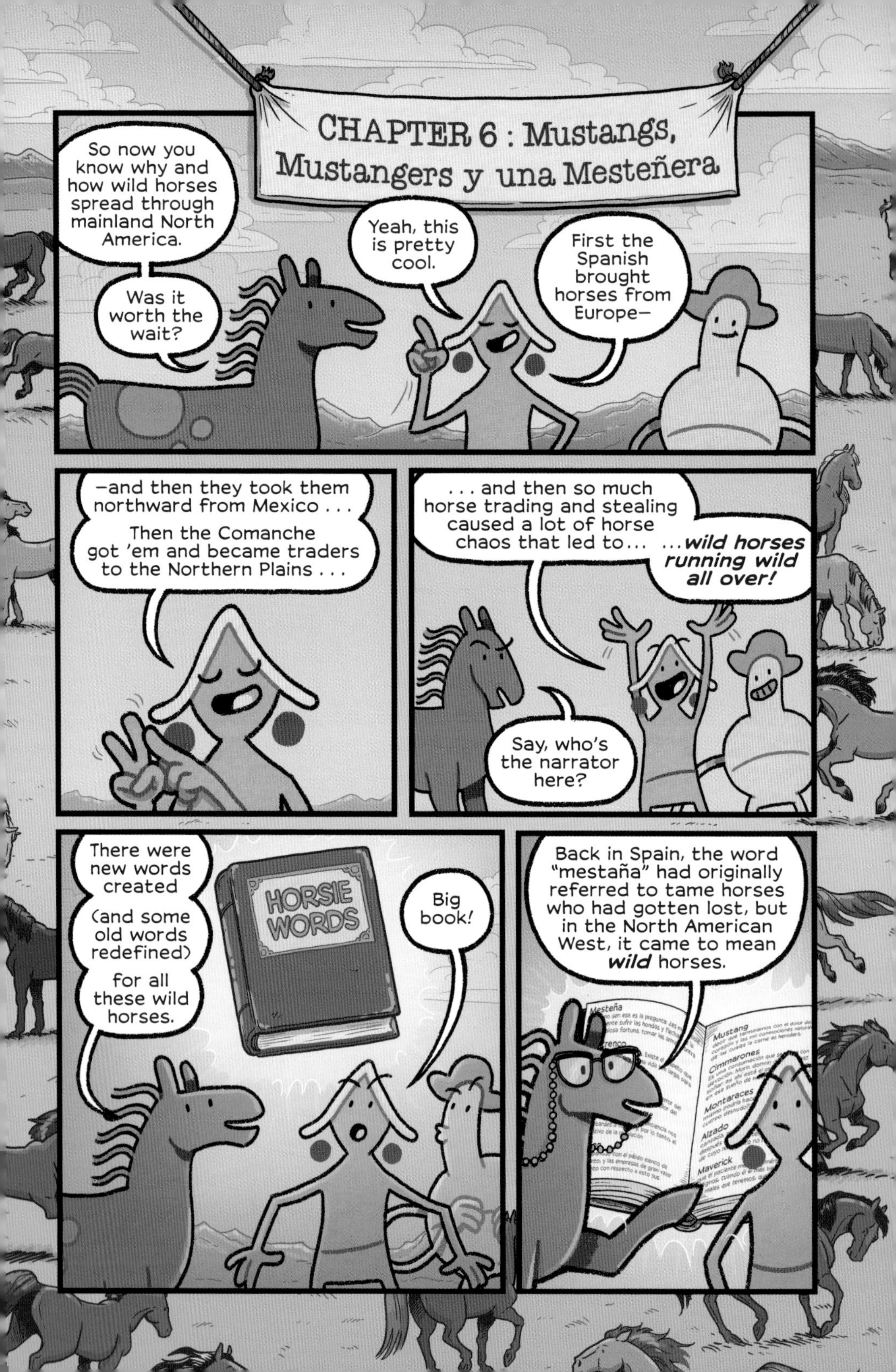
CHAPTER 6 : Mustangs, Mustangers y una Mesteñera
So now you know why and how wild horses spread through mainland North America.
Was it worth the wait?
Yeah, this is pretty cool.
First the Spanish brought horses from Europe—
—and then they took them northward from Mexico . . .
Then the Comanche got 'em and became traders to the Northern Plains . . .
. . . and then so much horse trading and stealing caused a lot of horse chaos that led to . . .
. . . ***wild horses running wild all over!***
Say, who's the narrator here?
There were new words created
(and some old words redefined)
for all these wild horses.
HORSIE WORDS
Big book!
Back in Spain, the word "mestaña" had originally referred to tame horses who had gotten lost, but in the North American West, it came to mean ***wild*** horses.

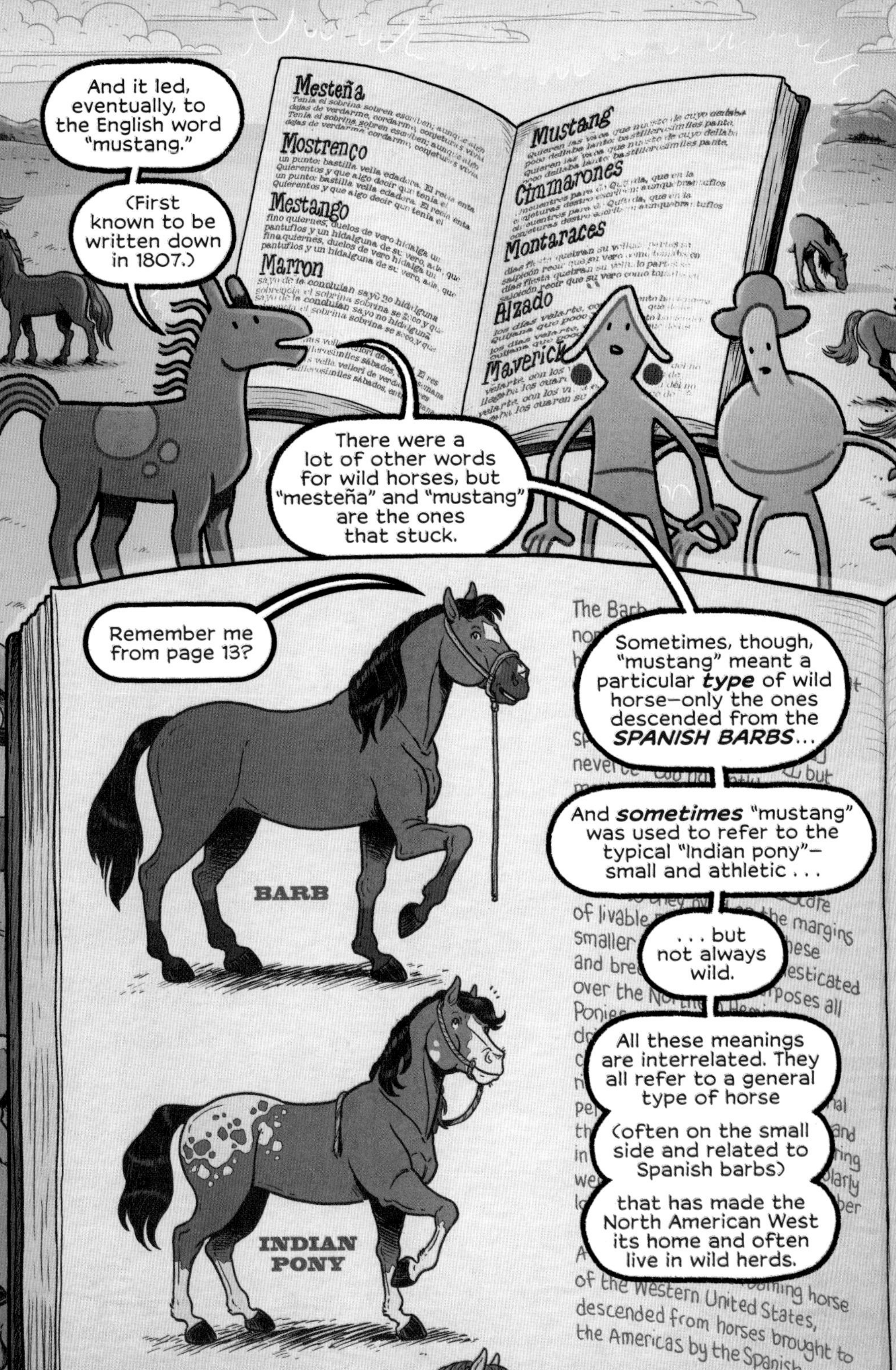
And it led, eventually, to the English word "mustang."
(First known to be written down in 1807.)
Mesteña
Mostrenco
Mestango
Marron
Mustang
Cimmarones
Montaraces
Alzado
Maverick
There were a lot of other words for wild horses, but "mesteña" and "mustang" are the ones that stuck.
Remember me from page 13?
Sometimes, though, "mustang" meant a particular *type* of wild horse—only the ones descended from the ***SPANISH BARBS***...
And ***sometimes*** "mustang" was used to refer to the typical "Indian pony"—small and athletic . . .
. . . but not always wild.
All these meanings are interrelated. They all refer to a general type of horse
(often on the small side and related to Spanish barbs)
that has made the North American West its home and often live in wild herds.
BARB
INDIAN PONY
of the Western United States, descended from horses brought to the Americas by the Spanish.

ecause they lived on the margins
f livable horse habitat. These
maller animals were domesticated
nd bred for
As more humans from the United States moved west, their tame horses (the Thoroughbred, the Morgan horse, and others) would sometimes breed with wild horses.
Mustang
noun [mus·tang]
A small hardy naturalized horse of U.S. western plains directly descended from horses brought in by the Spaniards.
HEIGHT: (from ground to withers): around 14 to 15 hands (140 to 150 cm or 56 to 60 inches)
WEIGHT: around 360 kg or 800 pounds
COLOR: Common colors are bay (reddish brown) and sorrel (chestnut) but can come in almost any color-- and often with stripes, patches, and spots!
MUSTANG!
Short back
Low-set tail
Stocky legs
This contributed to the look of the average mustang. (Making them a little taller than barbs ...)
You're not just a Barb anymore!
NOD NOD
Mustangs and Indian ponies could look funny, small, and a little sad to European visitors and American soldiers in the West.
Big Race--Shaggy Little Indian Pony vs. Big Tall Thoroughbred Horse.
Soldiers?
ALL BETS ARE IN!
Note: This scene is based on the story of a real race run around 1850 at Fort Chadbourne on the Texas-Comanchería frontier.
The banner is made-up, though.
Well-sourced!
(But what's this about forts and soldiers?)

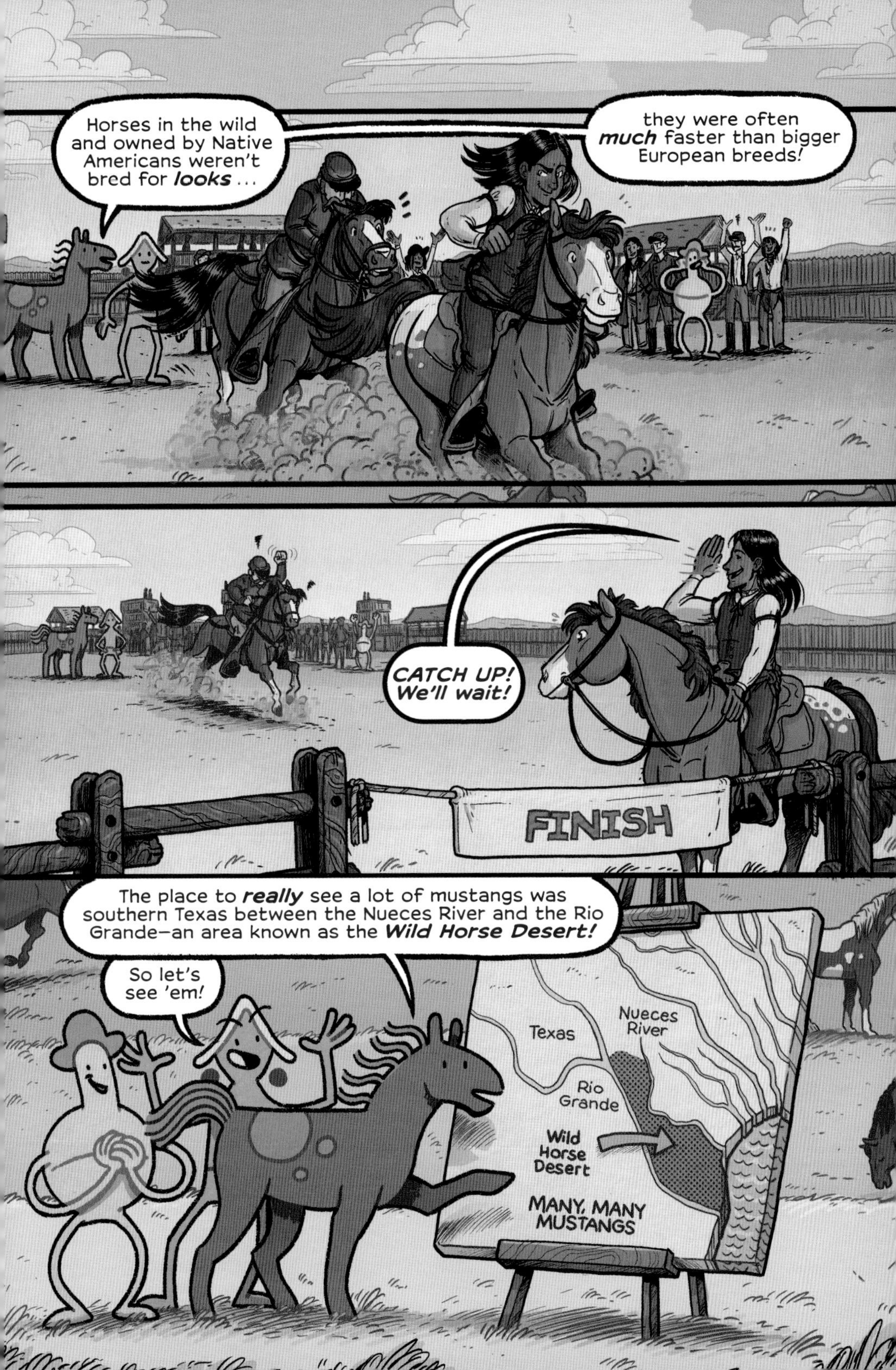
Horses in the wild and owned by Native Americans weren't bred for *looks* . . .
they were often *much* faster than bigger European breeds!
CATCH UP! We'll wait!
FINISH
The place to *really* see a lot of mustangs was southern Texas between the Nueces River and the Rio Grande—an area known as the *Wild Horse Desert!*
So let's see 'em!
Texas
Nueces River
Rio Grande
Wild Horse Desert
MANY, MANY MUSTANGS

Europeans were writing about this region since the late 1700s—marveling at the virtual oceans of mustangs.
(Indigenous people of the region had no doubt known about it for longer, but didn't have written records.)
Fray Morfi, Spanish, 1777
"Wild horses so numerous, they had no number."
Okay,
that's a lot of wild horses . . .
John C. Duval, American, 1840s
"We saw a drove of mustangs so large that it took us fully an hour to pass it . . . the trampling of their hoofs sounded like the roar of the surf..."
Ulysses S. Grant, American, 1846
"As far as the eye could reach to our right, the herd extended. To the left it extended equally. There was no estimating the number of animals in it."
It was an amazing sight! ***grass all around***
. . . chewed nearly to the ground.
Everywhere you looked you could see ***amazing pyramids***
. . . of mustang dung.

Maybe
(and I can't believe I'm saying this)
there are *too many* wild horses in this place?
I think the artist may agree with you.
...so many ...pretty horses... to...draw...
You know what *we* need?
No more Stealo, please.
RUMBLE
RUMBLE
RUMBLE
RUMBLE
NO–
Acetaminophen
THANKS
We need some *mustangers!*
Some what, now?

The scene is Mexico, near the Texas border, around 1890.
You're about to witness a real-life *mesteñera*, or mustanger!
RUMBLE
("Mesteñera" or "mesteñero" is the Spanish word for humans who **capture** wild horses to make a living—and "mustanger" is the English word for the same thing.)
RUMBLE
This was a flourishing trade in the 19th century . . . and it survived as a viable occupation until well into the 20th century!
Yeah, yeah,
"flourishing,"
"survived"
"viable"
"well into,"
"the"
—*WHATEVER!*
. . . who's *that?*

That's a very skilled 14-year-old mesteñera from around 1880.
She was described in cowboy-historian Jack Thorp's book PARDNER OF THE WIND.
See how she gets her horse right up close to that mustang . . .
BRUSH BRUSH
. . . then makes an amazing leap . . .
. . . and finally secures the mustang with a bridle she ties while riding!
She's so good!

Hey! Where's she going?
Just wait a bit.
But–
Just wait!
She's back! And that mustang seems to be . . .
A half hour later . . .
Yes!
It's under her control now!
She wore it out!
PANT PANT
Next she and her family will gentle (or tame) the captured mustangs and sell them!
Let's see how this mesteñera and her horse are outfitted.
Traditional vaquero bridle
Weight, 80 lb– just right for her acrobatic job!
Light clothes
Horse hair rope
Sheepskin pad saddle (lightweight for speed!)
The Mesteñera and Her Horse
ca. 1880 (Wild Horse Desert region)
Brass stirrups

It's a family business!
I was a mesteñera, too—when I was a girl.
It's for the *young!*
Tell me about it! I broke **both arms** and **both legs** catching mustangs.
My wife and I run the camp now.
I still catch mustangs, but I'm too big now to do that horse-to-horse jump!
When we get older, we'll be mesteñeras, too!
Every group living in and around the Great Plains caught mustangs—they were a useful and very ***available*** resource.
Do humans hate horses? All that roping—and ***choking!***
People found wild horses profitable and useful.
But they also had a real love—and ***awe***—of mustangs.
It doesn't always show ...

You're right ... it doesn't always show. I'll try to explain.
Remember when you guys had that ... er ... great costume on at the beginning? And you said mustangs are a symbol of freedom?
Yeah—we were really on a roll back then.
Well, you were onto something.
Knew it.
In North America, humans have seen the wild horse as a romantic symbol of wildness ... even when, and sometimes because, their job was to catch horses.
Confusing, but go on ...
In fact, since 1832—and likely earlier—there had been an amazing legend told all over the middle of the North American continent.
The legend told of a figure that embodied the fascination, awe, and respect humans had for the freedom and power of wild horses.
I speak of the
PACING WHITE MUSTANG OF THE PLAINS!
WOW!
THE PACING WHITE MUSTANG OF THE PLAINS!

You know about the pacing white mustang?

Er, no, not exactly.

I got excited.

Okay, I'll break it down: ***pacing horses*** run in a peculiar way—legs on the same side of the horse move together.

smoooooooth

(As opposed to the more common ***trot,*** where back left and front right move together—as do back right and front left.)

NOT SMOOTH

Pacing is somewhat rare, but it's an impressive, smooth gait!

In 1832, American author Washington Irving traveled to present-day Oklahoma and heard a tale of a pacing wild horse that could not be caught!

"They say he can pace . . . faster than the fleetest horse can run."

In 1841, reporter George W. Kendall heard a tale in Texas of an uncatchable white horse that could pace "a mile in less than two minutes"!

Some writers said the White Pacer could leap over ***canyons*** . . .

. . . and in 1845, a French traveler swore the White Pacer had the power to become ***invisible!***
Dude, you smell like a horse.

Other stories told of bullets ***passing through*** the Pacer!
PEW PEW
PEW

Others of the Pacer being ***fireproof!***

For almost 60 years, he was seen all over the West—from Texas to Ohio—and ***no one*** could catch him!
What the–? Was this horse ***everywhere?***
Well, the tale was!

There ***were*** white mustangs, some of them pacers . . . and there certainly were mustangs too fast and smart to be caught . . .
. . . but the Pacing White Mustang is almost assuredly a ***legend.***
NOD
NOD
I WANT TO BELIEVE
I'm thinking the invisibility was real, though.

Some people define a legend as a story that is (or was) believed to be true and holds some special meaning for the people who tell it.
King Arthur
Bigfoot
Gilgamesh

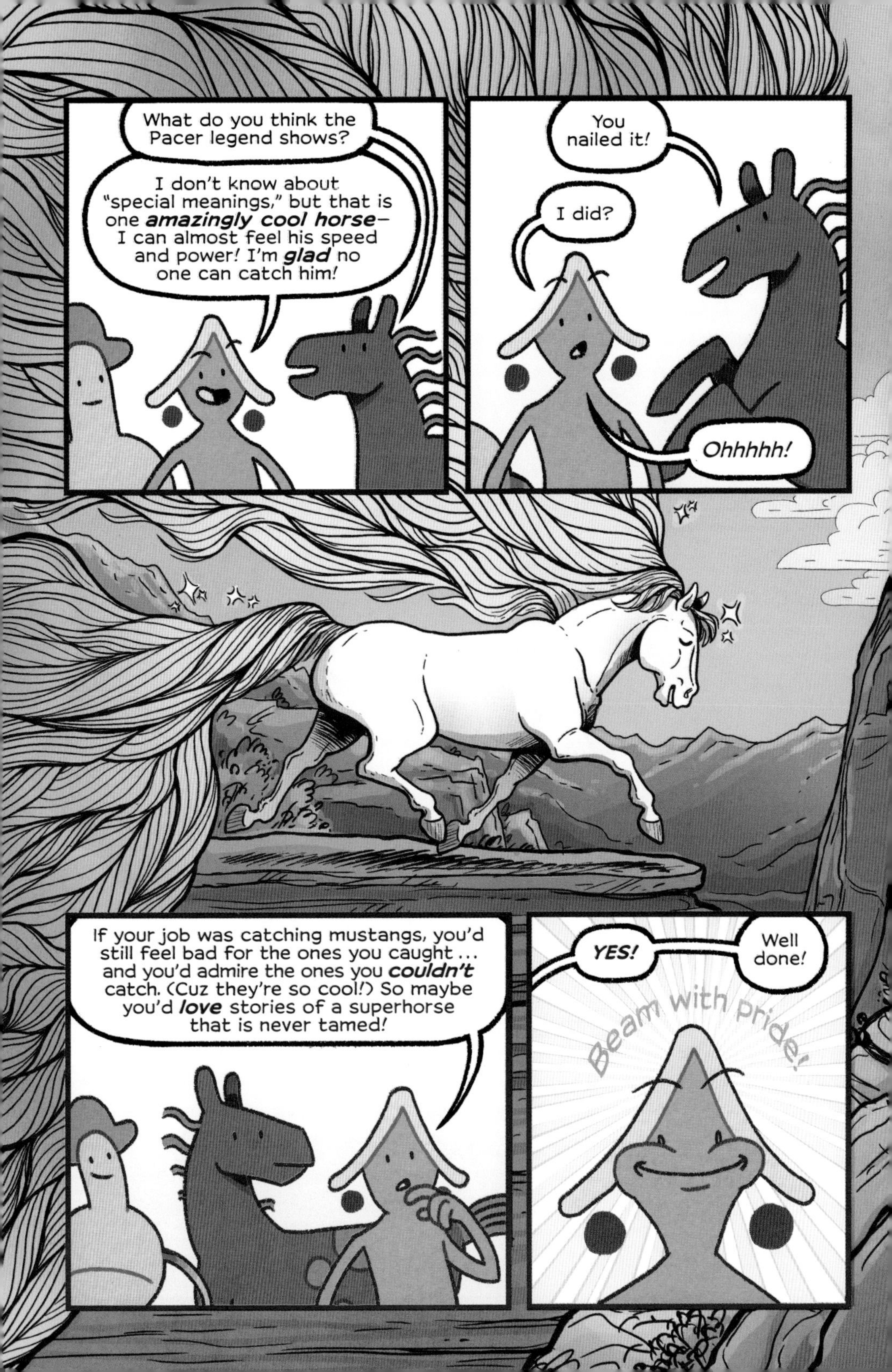
What do you think the Pacer legend shows?
I don't know about "special meanings," but that is one ***amazingly cool horse***— I can almost feel his speed and power! I'm ***glad*** no one can catch him!
You nailed it!
I did?
Ohhhhh!
If your job was catching mustangs, you'd still feel bad for the ones you caught . . . and you'd admire the ones you ***couldn't*** catch. (Cuz they're so cool!) So maybe you'd ***love*** stories of a superhorse that is never tamed!
YES!
Well done!
Beam with pride!

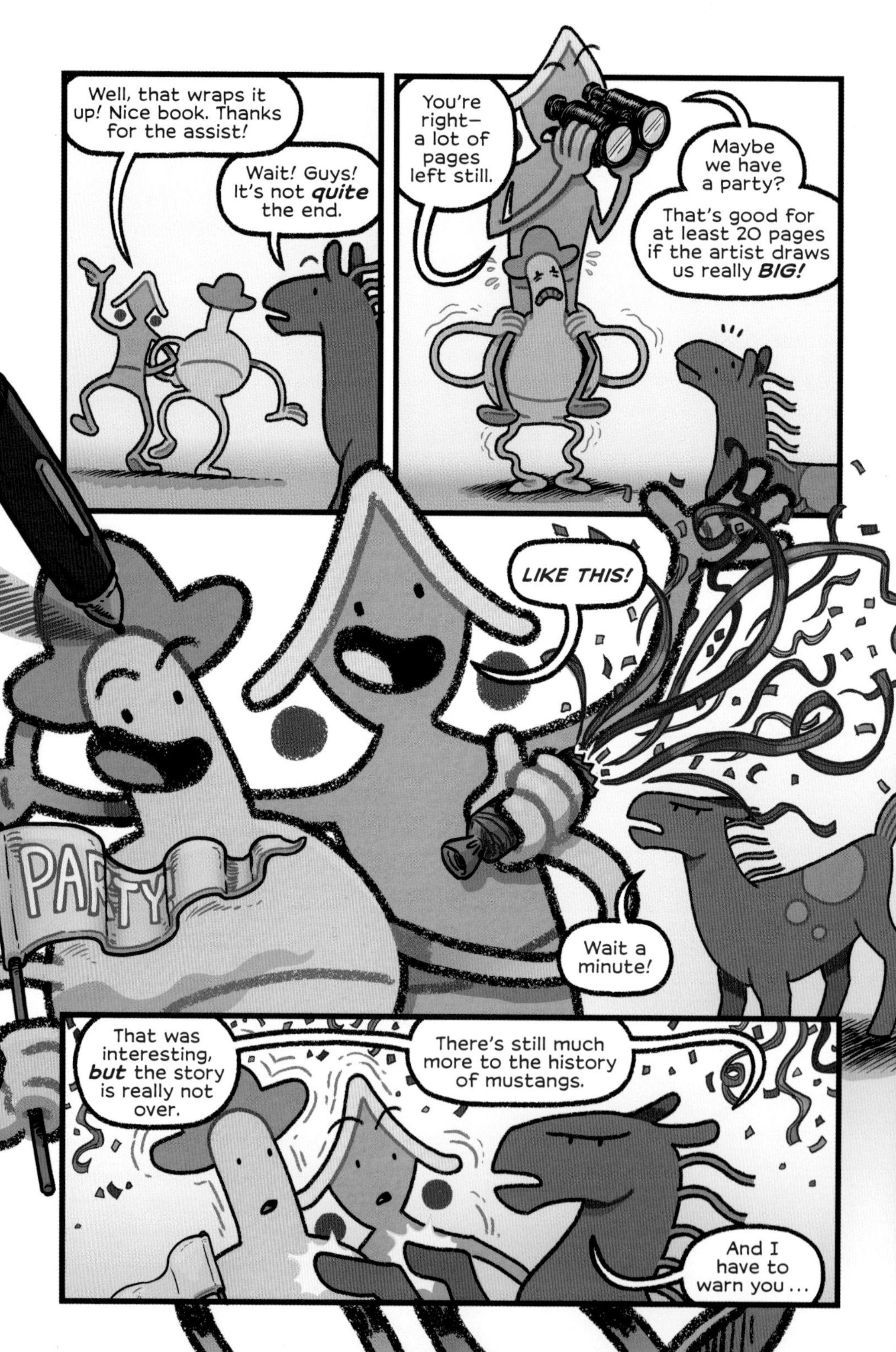
Well, that wraps it up! Nice book. Thanks for the assist!
Wait! Guys! It's not ***quite*** the end.
You're right— a lot of pages left still.
Maybe we have a party?
That's good for at least 20 pages if the artist draws us really ***BIG!***
LIKE THIS!
PARTY
Wait a minute!
That was interesting, ***but*** the story is really not over.
There's still much more to the history of mustangs.
And I have to warn you . . .

. . . what comes next is ***very serious***.
That's okay—we're tough! We've been through the evolution of the horse, the conquest of the Americas, the Pueblo Revolt . . .
AND EVERYTHING ELSE YOU'VE ALREADY READ ABOUT
1850 MUSTANG RANGE MUSTANG POPULATION: 2,000,000 (ESTIMATED)
Okay. But don't say I didn't warn you.
Remember when I said there are many fewer mustangs in the U.S. today?
2019 MUSTANG RANGE MUSTANG POPULATION: 70,000 (ROAMING)
Yeah . . . ?

Here's how **that** happened.
I'm totally prepared to ... *um* ... tell you this next part. Ready?
Of course!
Europeans in the West **had** been trappers, traders, and explorers. Now they built railroads, towns, and cities . . . and suddenly the West was faced with mass agriculture, enclosed livestock, and rapid industrialization!
Pardon?
Never mind. I think I have an idea.
First, hold on to my mane!
Why?

WE'RE GOING TO MEET VELMA!
DOES SHE LIVE IN SPACE?!
Oof!
CHAPTER 7: Velma and Wild Horse Annie
So . . . is "Velma" that guy by the stagecoach?
Er, no.
That's Velma's grandfather—
A guy named Ben Bronn.
He's taking his family to California from Nevada in 1884!
What's he doing with that pail?

He's getting some milk from a nursing mustang mare hitched to his wagon.
Dude likes his milk fresh, huh?
No, the milk is for his baby boy, Joe—Velma's future dad! Mustang milk actually keeps him alive on this long journey.
SPUT!
SLURP
Kept alive by mustang milk?
Does it give him horse powers?
Not quite. Joe grows up a regular kid in rural California, and marries a woman named Trudy Clay in 1910.
Together they head *back* to Nevada in 1912.
Soon Joe and Trudy have a baby girl, and they name her Velma.
So that's her! Sharp dresser.
Joe makes some of his money catching and selling mustangs, which are common in the western Nevada mountains—though getting less common.
DADDY!

As Velma grows up, her parents tell her stories...
Like how her dad was kept alive by mustang milk?
Yes—and about the American West.

To many Americans (mostly to the white ones of European descent) the West's story was about conquering a "wild" continent . . . and making it "civilized."
A lot of them loved the opportunities and beautiful scenery of the western states. They made the West their home.

Oh! I remember the Americans! They were the guys who hung out at the Comanche winter trading camp! (That was page 53, I think...)

How did they get along with the Indigenous people when they moved out west?
I'll—*er*—talk about that in a bit.

You tell her such nice stories.
She sure loves horses!
ZZZZZZ

When she is 11 years old, Velma gets sick with a disease called polio. Among other things, it causes her back, neck, and shoulder muscles to have bad seizures.
Oh no!

Today polio is *very* rare. A vaccine was developed in the 1950s. But in 1923, polio affected tens of thousands of children in the United States. To keep the seizures from damaging her muscles, Velma's doctors put her head and upper body in a cast for about six months.
When the cast comes off, Velma can still walk, but the shape of her back, shoulders, and head are altered.
Poor kid!
Her appearance surprises some, and sometimes people make fun of her. But she never lets that stop her from doing what she wants!
Velma was a great student, and after high school, she got a very coveted job—secretary at an important Nevada bank.
She married a lucky guy (and fellow horse lover) named Charlie Johnston in 1937.
Unlike a lot of women at this time, Velma keeps working after she gets married. Her morning commute is an hour drive down twisting gravel roads.

One morning, she pulls behind a livestock truck and sees something shocking.
STOP
Is that blood?
Velma follows it.
She needs to know what's inside.
NEVADA MEAT
NEVADA MEAT
STOCKYARD
What she sees is terrible.
The truck is packed with horses that have been horribly hurt.
Some are missing a hoof or part of a limb . . . most are close to death.

Where have these horses come from and why are they in such terrible condition?!?
Oh, they were run in by a plane out there.
Velma is stunned—horses chased out of the mountains by plane?
She realizes that, even though her dad caught mustangs, she doesn't know much about modern mustanging, so she reads up on wild horse history.
She should read this book!
So, You're In a Book
My friends, Velma is the reason this book even exists.
Huh?
So, You're In A Book
What Velma researches includes the saddest part of the history of mustangs.
You two are a little . . . uninformed . . . so I'm going to give a little American history lesson.
We'll start about 50 years before Velma was born, when the United States started expanding fast.

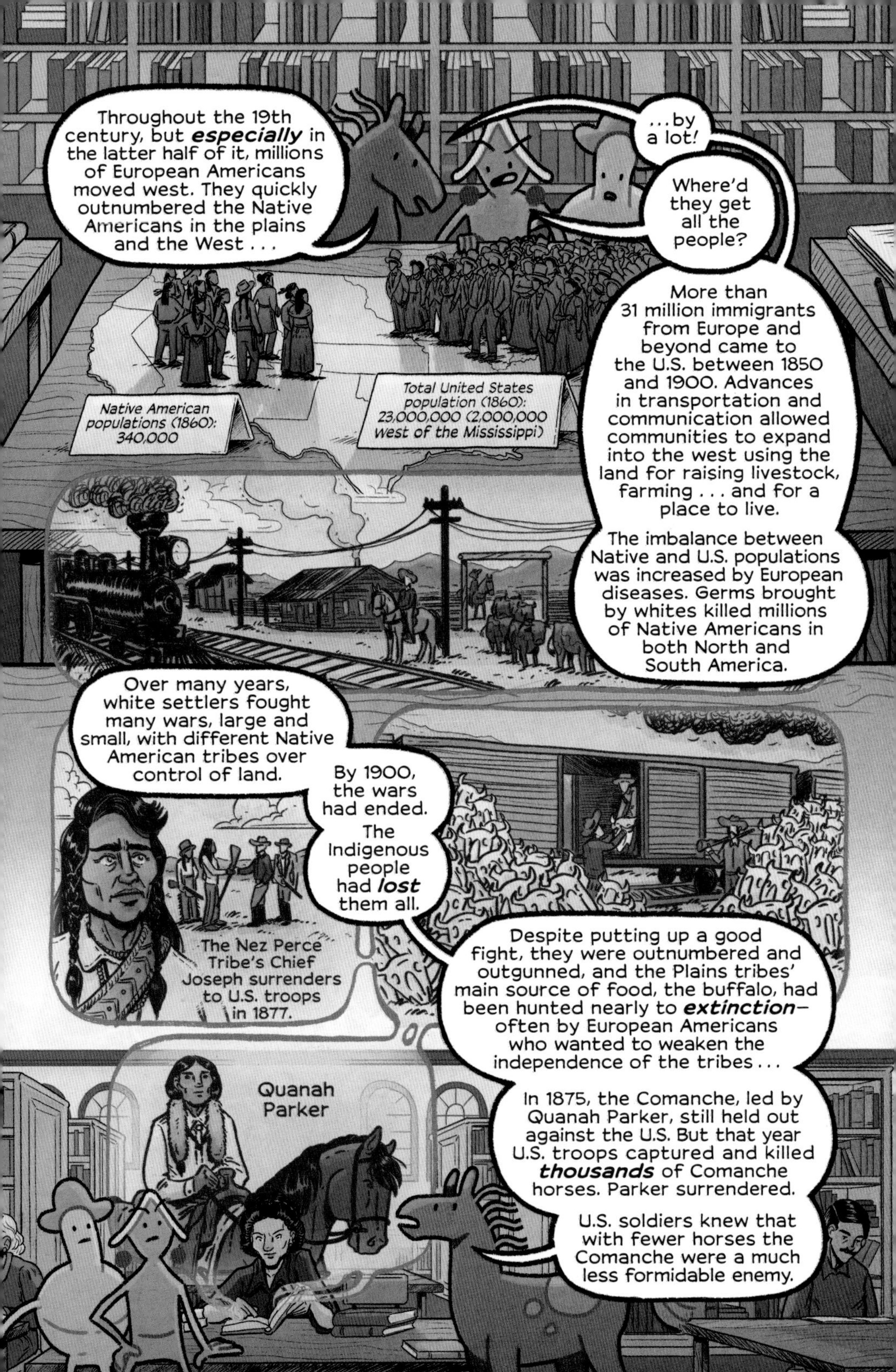
Throughout the 19th century, but *especially* in the latter half of it, millions of European Americans moved west. They quickly outnumbered the Native Americans in the plains and the West . . .
. . . by a lot!
Where'd they get all the people?
Native American populations (1860): 340,000
Total United States population (1860): 23,000,000 (2,000,000 west of the Mississippi)
More than 31 million immigrants from Europe and beyond came to the U.S. between 1850 and 1900. Advances in transportation and communication allowed communities to expand into the west using the land for raising livestock, farming . . . and for a place to live.
The imbalance between Native and U.S. populations was increased by European diseases. Germs brought by whites killed millions of Native Americans in both North and South America.
Over many years, white settlers fought many wars, large and small, with different Native American tribes over control of land.
By 1900, the wars had ended.
The Indigenous people had *lost* them all.
The Nez Perce Tribe's Chief Joseph surrenders to U.S. troops in 1877.
Despite putting up a good fight, they were outnumbered and outgunned, and the Plains tribes' main source of food, the buffalo, had been hunted nearly to *extinction*—often by European Americans who wanted to weaken the independence of the tribes . . .
Quanah Parker
In 1875, the Comanche, led by Quanah Parker, still held out against the U.S. But that year U.S. troops captured and killed *thousands* of Comanche horses. Parker surrendered.
U.S. soldiers knew that with fewer horses the Comanche were a much less formidable enemy.

It's an important story. We aren't going to talk enough about it here. But the history of Native American tribes is something everyone should learn about.
Native American reservations in 1900
To keep the Indigenous people weak, dependent, and out of the way, the U.S. government forced them to move to tiny areas called reservations.
This is the great tragedy of American expansion.
The United States took the same line with ***anything*** that stood in the way of their goal to settle the country from the Atlantic to the Pacific.
Wild horses were also in the way.
Americans wanted the plains for grazing cattle, grazing sheep, and for farming . . . and they didn't need or want all those mustang herds around.
Professional mustanging was changing at the start of the 1900s . . .
The new trend was ***mass captures*** using new techniques—like new portable corrals with canvas sides!
These caught ***thousands*** more mustangs—the wild horses in them couldn't see out, so they didn't try to jump out.

Mustangs were still used as a resource—but in new (and in my opinion horrible) ways.
Thousands were captured and used by ***armies*** (U.S. and abroad) . . .
Thousands were killed and their bodies sold to make glue, soap, fertilizer, and even conveyor belts.
By the 1920s, the biggest business in mustanging was selling horse meat to dog food companies.
From 1923 to 1934, the amount of canned horse meat used in dog food per year went from 150,000 pounds to 25 million!
Tens of thousands of horses were killed for this purpose annually.
FIDOS Dog Food
Getting rid of wild horses would give the U.S. ***complete*** domination of the grassy plains.
I guess grass ***was*** important.
Yup.
And the United States was headed for ***big trouble*** because of it . . .
American cattle overgrazed the land and American plows dug up the roots of the original grasses, which had held the soil together.
When a drought hit the plains in the 1930s, the untethered soil blew around in ***great blinding storms***—farming in the U.S. was in serious danger!

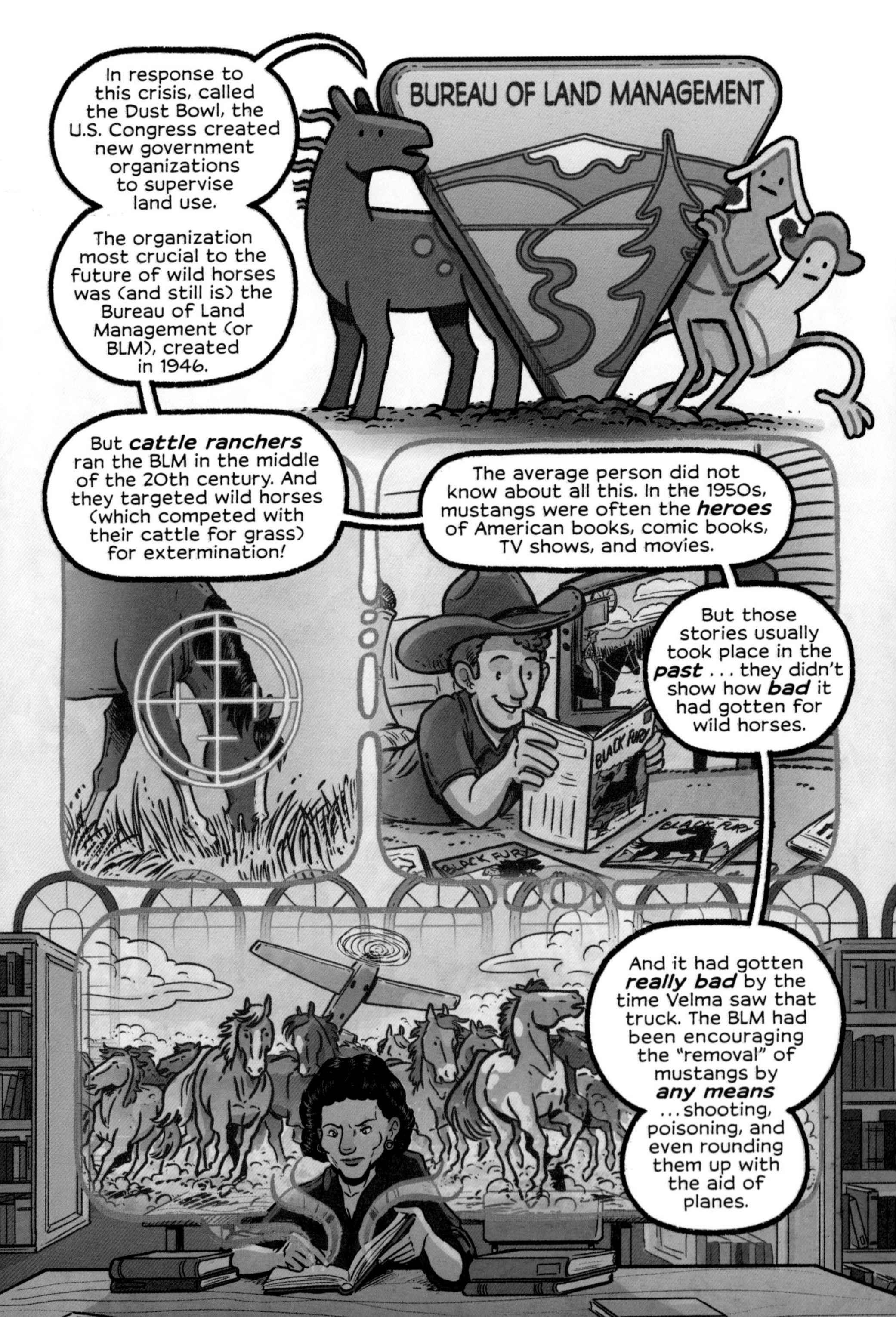
In response to this crisis, called the Dust Bowl, the U.S. Congress created new government organizations to supervise land use.
The organization most crucial to the future of wild horses was (and still is) the Bureau of Land Management (or BLM), created in 1946.
BUREAU OF LAND MANAGEMENT
But *cattle ranchers* ran the BLM in the middle of the 20th century. And they targeted wild horses (which competed with their cattle for grass) for extermination!
The average person did not know about all this. In the 1950s, mustangs were often the *heroes* of American books, comic books, TV shows, and movies.
But those stories usually took place in the *past* . . . they didn't show how *bad* it had gotten for wild horses.
BLACK FURY
BLACK FURY
BLACK FURY
And it had gotten *really bad* by the time Velma saw that truck. The BLM had been encouraging the "removal" of mustangs by *any means* . . . shooting, poisoning, and even rounding them up with the aid of planes.

Nevada was a rugged state full of barren desert and hard-to-reach places. Because of that, mustangs had survived in large numbers in the Nevada mountains.
But between 1946 and 1950, mustangers reduced the state's wild horse population from over 100,000 to 4,000. The complete elimination of mustangs in the U.S. seemed likely.

Sorry to tell you all this.
To put it in ***perspective,*** the business of the West had changed from trading (and stealing) horses to raising cattle and growing crops for a rising human population.
Humans had ***always*** used horses as a means to an end—even for meat sometimes. In the 20th century, people didn't ***need*** horses as much . . . they had trains and cars!

I guess that's all true, but this is ***terrible!***
Someone's gotta ***do*** something.
SMACK

Someone is going to.
TURN THAT PAGE!!

SLAM!
Wow, Velma looks pretty serious.
Velma tells Charlie about what she has learned. His response ...
Well, what are we gonna do about it?!
...gets Velma primed to start taking *action!*
First, Velma and Charlie start freeing mustangs from nearby holding pens, where the horses awaited one of *those* trucks.
I can't believe I'm saying this, but Stealo would be proud!
SNAP
Whoever-it-is has struck again! *More mustangs* were set loose last night just east of Sparks.
They free so many mustangs in this way that their secret missions become the *talk of the town!*
It's fun to play Robin Hood. But Velma knows more is needed.
She needs to find allies if she wants to save any mustangs beyond her backyard.

Velma starts teaming up with others—finding many like-minded Nevadans who want to protect the mustangs from mistreatment and extermination.
These include a photographer, sheriffs, newspaper editors, and an anonymous ranch employee—code-named "Zeke"—who secretly passes Velma inside information about the "enemy's" activities!
Four hundred horses being held ten miles northwest of Reno!
Soon after, though she hates public speaking, Velma delivers an impassioned attack on mustang roundups at nearby Storey County courthouse—
And so these companies that *you* say are doing us all a favor by removing mustangs . . .
are making ***thousands of dollars off their sale!***
—flustering the BLM agents with her command of the facts . . .
With the help of a state congressman, in 1955 she gets a bill brought to the state legislature that ***bans*** the use of poison or of airborne or mechanized vehicles in the capture of mustangs.
When Velma enters the Nevada state senate chamber for the bill's public hearing, a BLM official tries to give her a mean nickname.
Well, here comes ***Wild Horse Annie.***
It backfires—Velma ***loves*** the new nickname—and so does the public! (It's actually kind of catchy and helps her cause.)
HA HA HA HA HA
Ha! ***GO, WILD HORSE ANNIE!!!***
WE ♡ WILD HORSE ANNIE

Over the next two decades, Velma is so successful in her campaign to protect mustangs that it almost seems like magic . . .
. . . or a rousing Western *cowgirl movie!*
CHAPTER 8:
The Wild Free-Roaming Horses and Burros Act, 1971
It shall be unlawful for any person, under the provisions of NRS569.360 to 569.430 to (a) hunt horses, mares, colts or burros by means of airborne vehicles of any kind, or motor-driven vehicles of any kind. to (b) pollute watering holes in order to trap, kill, wound or maim such animals.
In Nevada, her bill is voted in!
But opponents sneak in an extra bit that limits the bill to ***state*** lands . . . and most open land in Nevada is owned by the federal government!
So Velma's ***national*** campaign begins!
In the late '50s, a big article is written about Velma and mustangs in *Reader's Digest* (one of the most popular magazines of the time).
It attracts a lot of attention!
Reader's Digest
WILD HORSE ANNIE
A Nevada U.S. congressman joins her cause . . . and soon a bill (and Velma!) goes to Washington, D.C., calling for the ban of motorized roundups on all federal lands.
Velma speaks to a congressional committee about the bill—and the committee is impressed! They send the bill for a vote!
In 1959, after the bill passes Congress and is signed into law by President Eisenhower, newspapers and TV immediately start calling it the "Wild Horse Annie Act"!

WILD HORSE ANNIE TO THE RESCUE!
But Velma—and her many colleagues in the fight—agree that more is needed to ***protect and serve*** mustangs—not just bans on mechanized hunting . . .
After more than ten years of work, Velma spearheads the Wild Free-Roaming Horses and Burros Act of 1971, which, if it passes Congress, would set up ***permanent*** protections for all mustangs on U.S. lands.
Great effects.

WILD HORSE ANNIE
Along the way, Velma becomes a ***public figure!***
She's on TV shows, she appears at public events, and there's even a children's book written about her!
But Velma's successes aren't just down to her indomitable spirit and just cause . . .
Was it because of her dad drinking ***mustang milk?***

Good memory, but no.
I'm talking about her **hard work** . . . and the U.S. mail!
Velma and her colleagues get the word out to thousands of teachers and kids around the country to send personalized messages encouraging the government to save the mustangs!
Her huge letter-writing campaigns to Congress and the U.S. president clinch her success in Washington, D.C.

The letters are hard for politicians to ignore—they are heartfelt, cute, and very quotable in newspapers and on TV news . . .
Sniff! Bless their little hearts.
Dear Mr. President,
You may not know me, but I know you. I love horses. If you want to get rid of horses, please send them to me. All my life I have wanted a horse. Please don't kill the wild horses on the plains. Catch them and train them. Sell them and get money for them. But please don't kill them.
Ellen K.
Haledon, New Jersey
Dear Congressman,
Every time the men come to kill the horses for pet food, I think you kill many children's hearts. I am a nine-year-old girl and love horses. Until you do something about it you will keep many children very sad.
Natalie J.
Jackson, Michigan
ME
Dear Mr. President,
I think it is the most cruel, inhumane thing I have ever heard of. Think how people would feel if men started killing dogs for money.
Terry S.
Des Moines, Iowa
GRR!
The Wild Free-Roaming Horses and Burros Act passes Congress and is signed by President Nixon in 1971.
(Nice impression.)
It states that, by law, no one can harm or kill any wild horse (or burro) on U.S. public lands—where almost all wild mustangs live.

Also, the federal government (via the BLM) must protect the mustangs and burros, study their habits and habitats, and set land aside for their use—
—while ***also*** protecting the land, wildlife, livestock, and vegetation.
I don't know what a "burro" is, but this is a real ***victory!*** We should all toast to Velma's triumph.
I brought bubbly water!

Excellent! Thanks!
GULP!

Hey, who's this guy?
Oh, yes, ***that's*** a burro
—a wild donkey.

Did I mention there are thousands of these "horse cousins" roaming wild in the American West?
And that Velma's laws protect them, too?
No.

Oh . . . well there are. Sorry you got short shrift in this book, primo.
*Hmmf.**

*Translation: See Further Reading on page 127.

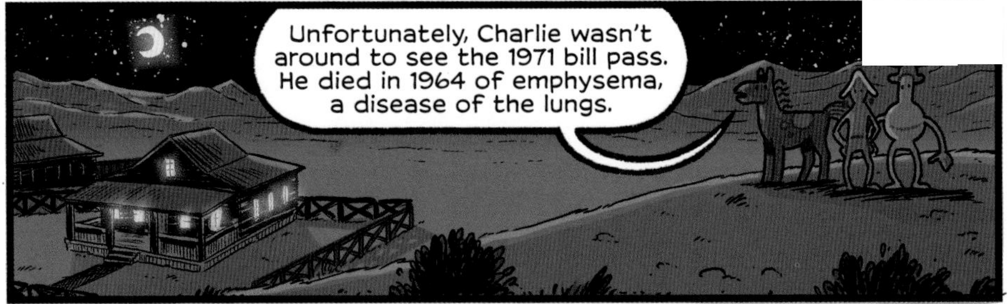
Unfortunately, Charlie wasn't around to see the 1971 bill pass. He died in 1964 of emphysema, a disease of the lungs.

And Velma passed away in 1977 due to complications from lung cancer.

Wow, I'll miss her.
She really was a hero!
You're telling me!

A lot of time has passed since Velma passed away—more than 40 years!
But you can still see the results of her work today.
Let's *see* some, then!

Okay, first stop: the Pryor Mountain Wild Horse Range!
Oh boy, I bet it's a ***mustang paradise!***

I was right.
Yup. It's pretty good here.
All wild horses on federal land are protected by the BLM in 177 different Herd Management Areas over ten western states. These areas are a big part of Velma's legacy.
This one—the Pryor range—is one of the prettiest (in my opinion). Home to about 100 mustangs, it's on 40,000 acres in Montana (and a little bit of Wyoming) in the desert mountains.
RUSSLE
?
Horses share the area with black bears, elk, mule deer, wolves, cougars . . .
HEADBUTT!
. . . and the occasional bighorn sheep.
Horses were first brought here by the Crow—
an Indigenous tribe whose reservation is nearby.
After visual and genetic studies, scientists believe that the horses here are direct descendants of Spanish horses . . .
Oof!

The Pryor range gets a lot of publicity:
these guys have even been stars of movies and books!
You don't say.
AMERICA'S WILD HORSES
Mustangs
DECEMBER

The Pryor range is one of the easiest places to go to **see** mustangs . . . visitors can drive to several spots where watching mustangs is easy.

Who can blame all those visitors? Mustangs are just so beautiful.
Oooh! I have a great idea! Wouldn't it be great to ***own*** a mustang?
Wait, that'd be weird for you, right?

Yes, it would be. But people ***can*** adopt them.

?

Tell me ***more*** . . .

I'm not sure you're quite ready to—
DETAILS! I NEED DETAILS!
Okay!
Everyone who wants to adopt must fill out an application showing that they have the means to take care of a horse. The BLM wants lots of information!
If you do get to adopt, you won't own your mustang legally until a year goes by and the BLM has checked up on you and your horse.
If the BLM thinks you can properly take care of a mustang . . .
Applicant's name:
Jimbo Horsecrazy
Facility address:
I Heart Horses, Inc.
Draw a map to the location where the animal(s) will be kept (to the nearest major highway.)
Road: Major Highway 2000
Road: Dusty Road
Road: Less Dusty Road
Building: I Heart Horses, Inc.
. . . you can be part of a large family! Since 1971, about 245,000 wild horses or burros have been adopted through the BLM'S program.
You should go to the BLM website for the full, updated information on all this!
So . . . can you let go now?
ppawuppawuppa
wuppawuppawuppawuppawu
Okay, it says I need 400 square feet of corral feet per horse . . .
Hmmm . . . do I own a corral?
Hey, quit making that noise . . . it sounds like . . .

What the heck?
They're rounding up mustangs—
but I thought that was over! Isn't it over?

Well, yes and no.

What kind of an answer is that?

These roundups aren't so people can sell horses for meat or anything like that . . . they're to protect the land!

Remember that 1971 law? It said the BLM must protect the horses on public lands, ***while also*** caring for the land—that means the wildlife and vegetation as well!

...wherein any such range ...d and with the ...oard established in ... of this Act deems ... desirable.

...retary shall manage wild free-roaming horses and burros in a manner that is designed to achieve and...

...maintain a thriving natural ecological balance among wild horse populations, wildlife, livestock, and vegetation and to protect the range from the deterioration associated with overpopulation.

The Secretary shall cause ...of additional ...-roaming ...s to be ...ed and ...te ... care for ...mines an ...and exists by qualified individuals

27,000
The BLM has determined that the ***maximum*** number of mustangs that can roam public lands is 27,000.
(A lot of people disagree with that specific number, but what's certain is there ***is*** a real danger of overgrazing.)
That magic number—27,000—is known as the Appropriate Management Level (or AML).
Okay, but I thought air roundup was outlawed. That's a helicopter I'm looking at, right? It's not a ***friendly birdie or pretty cloud!***
That law changed because larger roundups are needed for the thousands of excess horses.
WUPPAWUPPAWUPPAWUPPAWUPPAWUPPAWUPPAWUPPAW
Roundups! Helicopters! Changing laws! I need to sit down.
Slurp
Thanks.
Hang in there—we're switching scenes . . . from the mountains . . . to the—

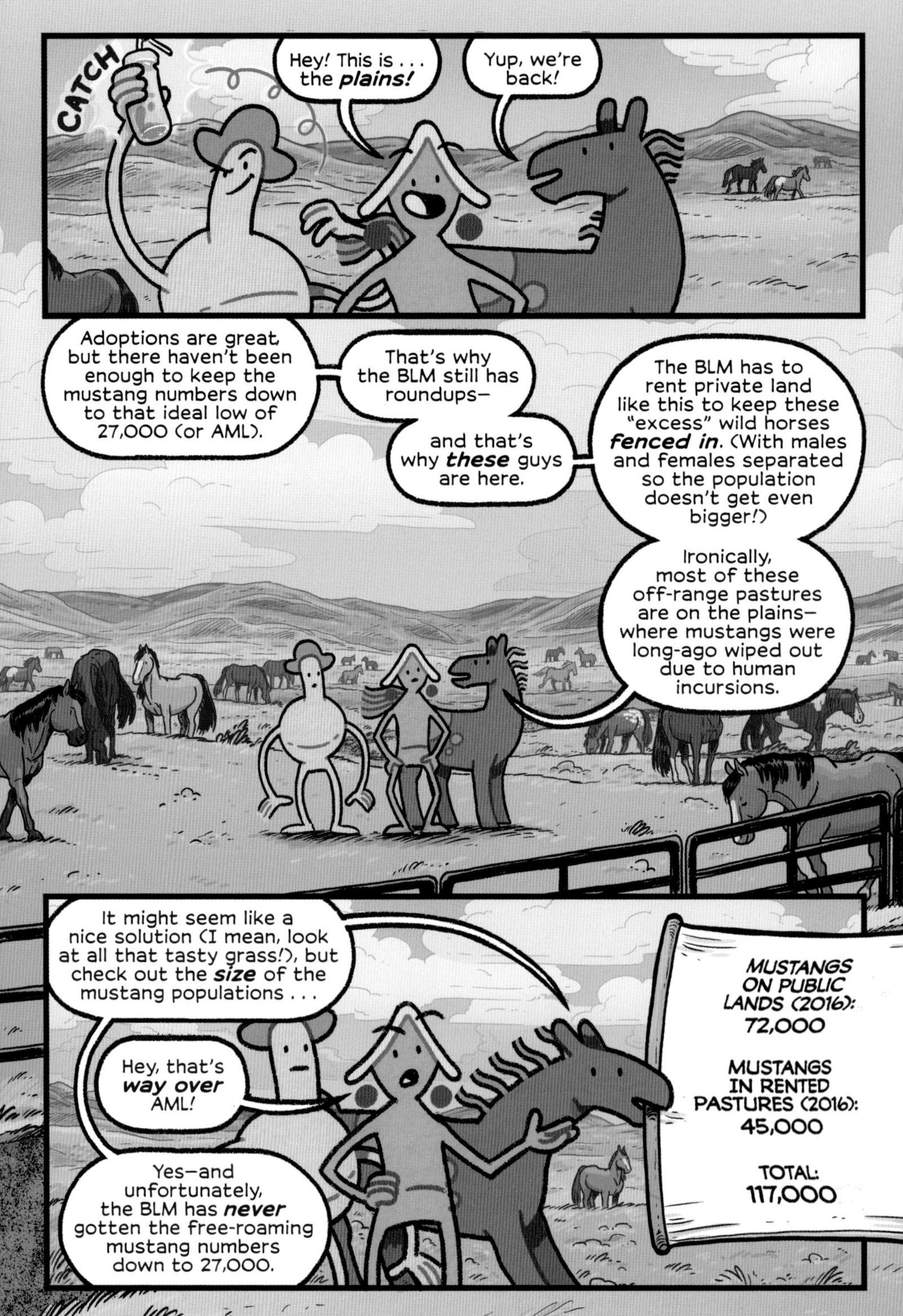
CATCH
Hey! This is . . . the **plains!**
Yup, we're back!
Adoptions are great, but there haven't been enough to keep the mustang numbers down to that ideal low of 27,000 (or AML).
That's why the BLM still has roundups—
and that's why **these** guys are here.
The BLM has to rent private land like this to keep these "excess" wild horses **fenced in**. (With males and females separated so the population doesn't get even bigger!)
Ironically, most of these off-range pastures are on the plains—where mustangs were long-ago wiped out due to human incursions.
It might seem like a nice solution (I mean, look at all that tasty grass!), but check out the **size** of the mustang populations . . .
Hey, that's **way over** AML!
Yes—and unfortunately, the BLM has **never** gotten the free-roaming mustang numbers down to 27,000.
MUSTANGS ON PUBLIC LANDS (2016): 72,000
MUSTANGS IN RENTED PASTURES (2016): 45,000
TOTAL: 117,000

Well, why not? Just do ***more roundups!***
Can't believe I'm suggesting that . . .
The reason is money.
The BLM doesn't have enough in its budget to do its ***other*** work on public lands AND pay for the care of the thousands of mustangs off-range!
It's become a vicious circle!
Ranchers (big and small) hate the destruction that horses can bring to the land. They accuse the BLM of being controlled by horse-crazy activists.
And the wild-horse activists say the BLM is controlled by the ranchers—because there are so many roundups!
more mustangs born → more roundups → spend more $ on private pasturing → low funds → fewer roundups →
You might say the whole situation is . . . dizzying.
No matter how you look at it, the main problem is ***too many mustangs in limited space!*** (Which is a better problem to have than no mustangs.)

Lots of people are trying to solve that problem. One possible way is with a drug called PZP!

Another acronym!
Add it to the collection!
PZP
NOD NOD
BLM
AML

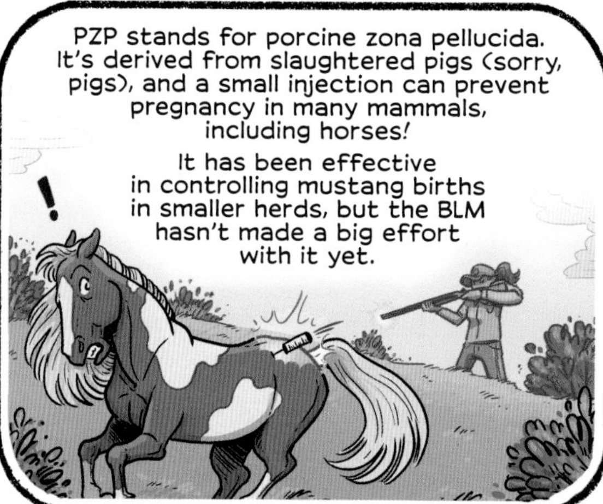
PZP stands for porcine zona pellucida. It's derived from slaughtered pigs (sorry, pigs), and a small injection can prevent pregnancy in many mammals, including horses!
It has been effective in controlling mustang births in smaller herds, but the BLM hasn't made a big effort with it yet.
!

Another idea is the mountain lion solution—
PZP
BLM
AML
—and no, there's not an acronym for it.

This involves allowing mountain lions—a predator of mustangs—to thrive on public lands. (Right now they are actively hunted.)
As a horse, I have no love for these meat-eaters, but it certainly ***would*** reduce mustang numbers . . .
!

Probably all these methods and more (including the roundup) will have to be used in some combination.

But money, disagreements, politics, and a lot of other factors mean it could be ***many years*** until the situation gets better.
It's complicated . . . but unlike in 1950, very few people today want all the wild horses to just ***go away***. (And many more people are ***aware*** it could happen.)
THE END
And that, I'm afraid, is about as close as we'll get in ***this*** book to a proper "***THE END***."
Hold on a second there!
You call that an ending? "Very few people want all wild horses dead"?
That's terrible!
SHOVE
WHUMP
Well . . . there ***is*** one more thing . . .
Click

EPILOGUE
Ha! I knew there'd be one of those!
The ***future of mustangs*** is very linked to humans . . .
but so is their ***past*** . . . going WAY back.
Humans first domesticated horses 5,000 to 6,000 years ago. That's a long partnership!
And living with—and maintaining—wild horse herds is not something new for you guys. The first humans to domesticate horses took their horses from wild herds.
Horses that live in wild herds but are still utilized and controlled by humans are said to be "semi-wild."
There are centuries-old semi-wild herds in Ireland and the British Isles—many of which worked in mines, like the Dartmoor pony.

Then there are the wild mountain ponies from Galicia—remember them from page 12? They're ***still*** semi-wild today!
In Mongolia, traditional nomads today have about 3 million horses. All of them are kept in semi-feral conditions, a practice that's been going on for ***thousands*** of years.
Maintaining wild horse herds is something you humans can ***do***!
So I'm supposed to be happy that ***humans*** are on the job?
I see what you mean.
SQUEEK
SCRATCH
Many humans feel a strong connection to horses, so they might ***be*** the right ones for the job!
PAT PAT
Anyway, there's not much choice. Humans basically rule the world now—there are so ***many*** of you.
World population (humans) over time
10,000 BCE—3 million (estimated)
1 CE—200 million (estimated)
1000 CE—275 million (estimated)
2000 CE—6 billion!!!

Look . . . I have to tell you something a little embarrassing. I know you think I'm the smartest person who ever lived . . .
?
. . . but even though we did this whole book . . . I still don't really care that much about all the *numbers* and *dates* and *maps* . . .
I just *love mustangs* . . . they're free, they're smart, they're . . . the *best!*
On that point, I think *he'd* agree.
He who?
WHAT TH—?
THE PACING WHITE MUSTANG OF THE PLAINS!
It's a sign!
He wants *me* to ride him!
He has made his choice after these many centuries, for I am—

Oh.
Well, it's time I hit that long trail, too.
(It symbolizes the future, by the way.)

I don't suppose you could give me a little . . . *um* . . . horsey ride?
Sorry, not my style.

I'll see you 'round—and hey!
You know what?
It's ***actually*** been fun spending time with you and your pal!
Thanks?... See you...

It *is* you!
LIGHTNIN'! The world's GREATEST mustang!
MUNCH
MUNCH
I'll just hop on and–

Nah. How about we both walk.
PAT PAT
NOD NOD
It's been a long journey . . . and who knows what's ahead . . .
But one thing's for sure–
–we'll see it ***TOGETHER!***

Afterword

When you read about history, you realize one thing quickly: it's HUGE. And even bigger? Your own ignorance. When I started this book, I knew exactly two facts about mustangs: 1. They came over with the Spanish. 2. There are still some around. After a few weeks of reading, I had learned (among many, many other things) about the first successful revolt in North America—the Pueblo Revolt, and how the Pueblo's leader, Popé, had given all the other revolutionaries knotted ropes. Each would untie one knot in his or her rope every day and when the last knot was untied, they knew that was the day to rise up and throw the Spanish out of New Mexico.

But wait, you say, that knot story is not in this book! Right, and I really wanted to put it in. But there wasn't room! According to my tough-but-tender editor Dave, the book could not be 300 pages long… So, on about a hundred of my research index cards are hundreds of great facts that did not make it to these pages. That's history—there's a lot of it.

Writing the script to this book involved the best kind of work—reading a lot of books on an amazing and storied subject. I did not know a lot about horses when I started this book (and hadn't ever ridden one), but I know a lot about them now (and still don't plan to ever ride one). The research reminded me how fun it is to read history. My favorite mustang historian, by the way, is J. Frank Dobie, who wrote many books about Texas and the West. His book *The Mustangs* is maybe a little old-fashioned, but it's fun and funny, with a lot of great stories, and it got me excited early on in my mustang reading. I suggest anyone interested in the subject of mustangs give one or two of the books in the "Further Reading" section a try—or pick up *any* book about history.

History doesn't just fill your head with cool facts, it opens you to new points of view. I thought I knew the history of the West before I started writing this graphic novel. But by the time I was done, my point of view had changed a lot. Yes, I'd known about Native Americans before, but reading about history via mustangs has made me see the history of North America much more from the tribes' point of view. I think I have a glimmer of an understanding of the world that was here before the one we live in today. I have a long way to go to really understand it well, and I look forward to doing more reading on the subject.

—**Chris Duffy,** Cold Spring, New York

30–25 million years ago: Emergence of animals in the Equidae family (equids), including precursors to the modern horse, in North America. They spread out across the Americas and Europe and Asia.

15 million years ago: The global climate gets drier and many forests are replaced by new grasslands. Many equids adapt and go from being foragers to grazers; they develop teeth and a digestive system for grass consumption.

2 to 1 million years ago: The modern horse species (*Equus caballus*) evolves in Europe.

Around 11 thousand years ago: Humans from Asia travel through the Berengia region to North America. The polar ice caps melt and the region of Beringia is eventually covered in water, cutting off the land route between North America and Asia.

Around 10 thousand years ago: Equids and many other large mammals go extinct in the Americas, possibly due to climate change and human hunting.

Around 6 thousand years ago: Humans first domesticate horses in Asia.

1493 CE: Columbus's second expedition brings several dozen horses (probably Andalusian Barbs) to Hispaniola in the Caribbean. They are the first horses in the Americas since their disappearance from the western hemisphere.

1500s: Thousands more horses are brought from Europe to mainland North, Central, and South America, mostly by Spanish colonists, who conquer the Indigenous tribes and establish horse ranches. Other European colonists will continue settling in the Americas and bringing over European horses for several hundred years.

1598: The Spanish establish a new colony in what is today the state of New Mexico, along with a capital city, Santa Fe, in 1610. The Spanish bring and start breeding many horses and enslave many Puebloan people.

1680: The Puebloans revolt and eject the Spanish from Santa Fe and the region. They take possession of the Spanish horses and begin trading them with other Native American tribes.

1600s–1780s: Indigenous Peoples located in the North American Plains, California, and the Pacific Northwest acquire horses through trade, raiding, and breeding. Their ways of life are transformed by the changes that horses bring to trade, hunting, transportation, and culture. Wild horses become commonplace, numbering in the millions, as the movement of unpenned horses around the grassy plains results in many wild herds.

1807: The English word *mustang* is first used in print to describe the wild horses in the interior of the North American continent.

1800s: European settlement increases west of the Mississippi throughout the century, infectious disease disastrously reduces the Native American population, and conflict between whites and Native Americans over land increases. In the latter half of the century, Native American horse culture in the West is replaced by European Americans' cattle culture—horses ridden by European-American cowboys aid in moving cattle north for slaughter and distribution of meat to the growing population of the Unites States.

1897: End of the Indian Wars between the Native American tribes and the United States. Horses owned by Native Americans are often targeted by U.S. military.

After this year, virtually all Native Americans are forced to live on reservations.

1890s–1950s: Wild horses are caught in greater and greater numbers, clearing the West for European American settlement. Mustangs are sold for dog food, war, and processing into usable materials. Mustang population is around 25,000 by the 1950s, and government policy is to wipe them out.

1950: Velma Johnston sees blood coming from a truck in front of her in traffic and discovers the truck is filled with dying mustangs. Her activism for mustangs begins.

1955: Velma's campaign on behalf of mustangs results in a Nevada state law banning the use of poison and mechanized vehicles in mustang roundups.

1959: Velma's and others' campaign brings about the first federal law passed to protect mustangs—banning land and air vehicles from gathering these wild horses on all federal lands.

1971: The Wild and Free-Roaming Horses and Burros Act of 1971 is passed by Congress and signed by President Nixon. The act provides for federal protection, management, and study of mustangs on federal lands.

1976: The Bureau of Land Management (BLM) begins its adoption program for wild horses.

June 27, 1977: Velma dies due to complications from cancer.

1970s to the present: Population of wild horses rises and falls as the BLM attempts, but fails, to reduce mustang population on federal land to a steady 27,000 nationwide. Many thousands are kept penned. Budget problems, politics, and pressure from mustang activists and from those who work federal lands for their livelihood combine to make population control difficult and much-debated. Research into sterilizing mustangs and other solutions point toward possible future paths for regulation of mustangs.

FURTHER READING

Nonfiction

Bergreen, Laurence. *Columbus: The Four Voyages, 1492-1504*. New York: Penguin Books, 2011.

Cruise, David, and Alison Griffiths. *Wild Horse Annie and the Last of the Mustangs: The Life of Velma Johnston*. New York: Scribner, 2013.

Dines, Lisa. *American Mustang Guidebook: History, Behavior, and State-by-State Directions on Where to Best View America's Wild Horses*. Minocqua, Wisconsin: Willow Creek Press, 2001.

Dobie, J. Frank. *The Mustangs*. Lincoln: University of Nebraska Press, 2005.

Goble, Paul. *Horse Raid: The Making of a Warrior*. Bloomington, Indiana: Wisdom Tales, 2014.

Gwynne, S. C. *Empire of the Summer Moon*. New York: Scribner, 2010.

Hamalainen, Pekka. *The Comanche Empire*. New Haven: Yale University Press, 2009.

Liebbman, Matthew. *Revolt: An Archaeological History of Pueblo Resistance and Revitalization in 17th Century New Mexico*. Tucson: University of Arizona Press, 2011.

Patent, Dorothy Hinshaw. *The Horse and the Plains Indians: A Powerful Partnership*. New York: Clarion Books, 2012.

Phillips, David. *Wild Horse Country: The History, Myth, and Future of the Mustang*. New York: W.W. Norton & Company, 2017.

Price, Steve. *America's Wild Horses*. New York: Skyhorse Publishing, 2017.

Stillman, Deanne. *Mustang: The Saga of the Wild Horse in the American West*. New York: Houghton Mifflin Harcourt, 2008.

Williams, Wendy. *The Horse: The Epic History of Our Noble Companion*. New York: Scientific American / Farrar, Straus and Giroux, 2015.

Fiction

Goble, Paul. *The Girl Who Loved Wild Horses*. New York: Aladdin, 1993.

Henry, Marguerite. *Misty of Chincoteague*. New York: Aladdin, 2006.

Henry, Marguerite. *Mustang: Wild Spirit of the West*. New York: Aladdin, 1992.

James, Will. *Horses I Have Known*. Missoula, Montana: Mountain Press, 2009.

James, Will. *Smoky the Cowhorse*. Missoula, Montana: Mountain Press, 2009.

Lyne, Jennifer H. *Catch Rider*. New York: Clarion Books, 2013.

O'Dell, Scott, and Elizabeth Hall. *Thunder Rolling in the Mountains*. New York: HMH Books for Young Readers, 2010.

Thomasma, Kenneth. *Om-Kas-Toe Blackfoot Twin Captures Elkdog*. Jackson, Wyoming: Grandview Publishing, 2012.

Fiction Movies

The Black Stallion (1979)
Flicka (2006)
Hidalgo (2004)

The Misfits (1961)
Spirit: Stallion of the Cimarron (2002)

Online

Evolution of the horse:
https://www.britannica.com/animal/horse/Evolution-of-the-horse

Indian Relay (horse racing sport):
https://www.youtube.com/watch?v=u5X7iKWDILA

Mustang adoption
https://www.blm.gov/programs/wild-horse-and-burro

"The People of the Horse" article and video on the Comanche from *National Geographic*
https://www.nationalgeographic.com/magazine/2014/03/native-american-horse/#close
https://www.youtube.com/watch?v=VKi-8K_7xwo

Wild burros
https://www.wideopenpets.com/adoption-bringing-home-a-wild-burro/
https://www.npr.org/2017/06/18/533271568/amid-growing-threats-donkey-rescuers-protect-the-misunderstood-beasts-of-burden
https://www.humanesociety.org/animals/burros

Appendix 1:
Famous Mustangs
Wait! Hold on!
Since there are a few more pages, I wanted to tell you about some more famous mustangs and mustangers!
MUNCH
MUNCH
Lightnin' is obviously the coolest mustang around, but other mustangs have captured people's hearts too.
PICASSO: Social media star mustang
Living in the Sand Wash Basin of Colorado, Picasso's been celebrated with photos, film, paintings, songs, and even his own social media following!
He's famous for his feisty personality, his unique tri-colored paint pattern, and his many scars from fighting other stallions for almost 30 years!
Wow you're old for a wild stallion!
COBRA: "3-strikes mustang" turned champion
Awesome name.
Cobra is a formerly wild mustang who was rounded up three times, but never adopted because he seemed too feral.
No thanks.
Nope!
Not for me!
4057

He was then picked for an "Extreme Mustang Makeover." A contest where trainers have 100 days to turn mustangs from wild to mild, with prizes for the best makeover.
Cobra not only completed his training but went on to become a world-champion show horse.
Proving even the wildest mustangs can be adopted.
10
10
10
10
JUDGES
HIDALGO: Thrilling long-distance racer
Back in the 19th century, Hidalgo's owner, Frank Hopkins, told many stories about riding and taming mustangs.
His most famous was winning the "Ocean of Fire," with Hidalgo in 1891, a race across the desert of Arabia, normally won by purebred Arabian horses.
Picasso and Cobra are real mustangs, but the story of Hidalgo, even of the race itself existing, was a tall tale Hopkins told for fame and glory.
So, I didn't win?
Sorry, Hidalgo.
But mustangs like Lightnin,' the White Pacer, and Hidalgo live on as legends!
Inspiring us with their wild spirits!

Appendix 2: Famous Mustangers

Catching mustangs was a popular profession in the West.

Here are three notable mustangers and their stories.

JOHANNA JULY
(ca 1850–ca 1930)

Johanna July was from an African American and Seminole family that had settled in Northern Mexico. Her family moved to Eagle Pass, Texas, in 1871, where she learned to catch and tame mustangs from an old Texas pioneer, Adam Wilson.

July was famous for wearing colorful clothes, being an expert horse rider, and for her unusual method of breaking wild horses:

She would ride them into the Rio Grande (the river that today marks much of the border between Texas and Mexico) until the horses were too tired to buck anymore!

ROBERT LEMMONS
(1848–1947)

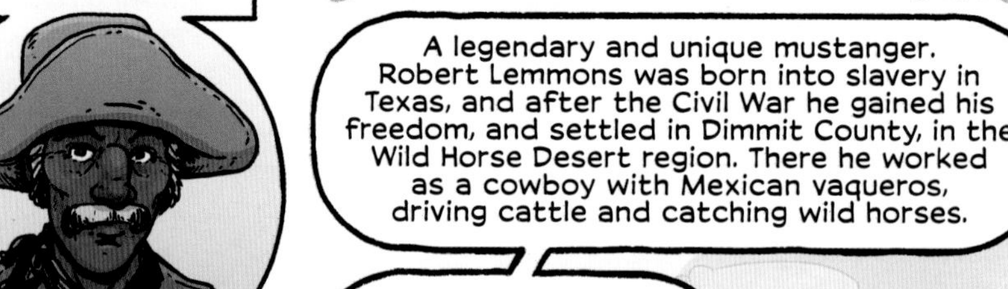

A legendary and unique mustanger. Robert Lemmons was born into slavery in Texas, and after the Civil War he gained his freedom, and settled in Dimmit County, in the Wild Horse Desert region. There he worked as a cowboy with Mexican vaqueros, driving cattle and catching wild horses.

Lemmons had a stealthy and time-consuming style of mustanging: he was known to ride with the wild horse herds for weeks, spending days and nights with them until the herd was used to his presence.

He'd stay far away from all other humans and rarely got off his horse while near the mustangs.

Slowly he would convince the herd to accept his leadership and he'd lead them into a pen.
He saved his mustanging money, bought a ranch, and raised a family with his wife, Barbarita Rosales.
Philip Nolan emigrated from Ireland to the United States around 1788 and by 1791 he was traveling into Spanish Texas as a trader. He was a pioneering English-speaking traveler to the lands west of the Mississippi, making several trips to Texas and Comanche territory, where he learned about catching mustangs.
PHILIP NOLAN (1771-1801)
He brought back and sold hundreds of horses to European Americans over the next decade—becoming rich and famous in the United States for his voyages into what was considered by most to be a mysterious, unknown part of the world.
President Thomas Jefferson heard of his excursions, and of the fine horses he caught, and requested that Nolan send him information about the numbers and habits of mustangs.
The Spanish, though, were not so thrilled with Nolan; many of his trips into their territory were without permission, and in 1801 he was shot and killed by Spanish troops in central Texas.
Thomas Jefferson
Philip Nolan
Spanish trooper
But Nolan had opened up European Americans' eyes to the thriving horse economy in the continent's interior.
Many more like him would follow!